Nothing on the Field

A message of hope from a recovering anorexic

by

Eileen Rand

Chase Enterprises Publishing

ISBN-13: 978-1-927915-06-6 (Print Edition)
ISBN-13: 978-1-927915-07-3 (e-book)

Published Dec 1st , 2014
Chase Enterprises Publishing
Box 2922, Kenora, ON, Canada P9N 4C8

Additional copies may be purchased at:
http://shop.claytonbye.com

Visit us at:
www.claytonbye.com

Acknowledgements

My mother Elise Rand, my Godmother Emma Lee Phelan, Mary Cavelli Johnson, Jeff and Jackie Rand, Clayton Clifford Bye, Dr. Chandler Chang, Tammy Holcomb, Page Love, Lisa Davis my dietician, Miss Jenna and Miss Geri at The Karis Home, Dr. Michael Strober, Maureen Lynch and the entire staff at UCLA, Dr. Cindy Pikus, Elizabeth Bailey, Dr. Terry Schwartz, Dr. Philip Botkiss at UCSD, Gene Fitzpatrick, Mary Ellen Trunko, Kris Shock and everyone who helped me along the way.

Table of Contents

The Purpose of this Book

Eileen Rand

I want to let people know that those who suffer from such conditions as Bulimia and Anorexia are not castaways to be left on the *Island of Misfit Toys*.[1] Too many books make light of these disorders or diseases. Some even glorify them. Not me. This will be a raw account of what it's like to live with and die from eating disorders.

In this book you'll find the account of a friend of mine who died at age 22 of complications extending from Anorexia. But her life wasn't a waste, for she and her mother loved each other unconditionally. This woman, Mary, stuck with her daughter when many said to just let her go. God saw that she was rewarded with a good friend who understood what Mary was going through. That friend? She was my mother, and they stayed friends for many years, until my mother died in September, 2013.

My mother. Yes, she understood the disease, because she too refused to give up on her daughter;

[1]http://en.wikipedia.org/wiki/Rudolph_the_Red-Nosed_Reindeer_and_the_Island_of_Misfit_Toys

her love was unconditional. And if there can be any message at all in a story where some get well, many don't, and others even die, it must be that love is the only thing that heals.

There's a second purpose in the words that follow. I'd like to raise awareness that there are no longer-term assisted living homes for people like myself for whom the condition seems to be more permanent. My vision for such a facility would include a supportive team to help the bulimic or anorexic maintain the progress obtained during her time in intensive treatment. Leaving intensive treatment, halfway house support or even outpatient follow up—to go out on your own again—is a set-up for relapse. It creates a void in which the anorexic has to monitor her own eating habits, curb her fanatic need to exercise and try to manage her OCD (Obsessive Compulsive Disorder) behaviors, all by herself. This is usually doomed to failure. No, what's required is a place or places where an Anorexic can go to live on a permanent basis until or if she becomes well. This would be modeled after regular assisted living homes, but the dietician on staff would be well versed in the needs of the Anorexic. The staff and director would have to have similar credentials. And the whole culture would be centered around supporting the Anorexic in her quest to become well.

Note that I wrote "supporting the Anorexic." There would be no punitive measures such as those found in hospitals like Johns Hopkins. Treatment would be based on love, respect and the genuine wish to HELP the Anorexic get well rather than the strictly behavioral approach in which forced feeding and forced weight gain are employed.

Important Definitions

Definition of ANOREXIA NERVOSA:

A serious eating disorder, mostly in young women, characterized by a failure to maintain body weight at a normal level because of an intense desire to be thin, a fear of gaining weight, or a disturbance in body image. Anorexia nervosa typically begins in late adolescence, and a usual symptom in women is AMENORRHEA. A person with this disease will often go to great lengths to resist eating in order to lose weight, and medical complications can be life-threatening. Treatment can include psychological and social therapy.[2]

Definition of AMENORRHEA:

Lack of MENSTRUATION. Signs of primary amenorrhea (failure to start menstruating by age 16) include infantile reproductive organs, lack of breasts and pubic hair, dwarfism, and deficient muscle development. In secondary amenorrhea (abnormal cessation of cycles once started), the genitals atrophy and pubic hair diminishes. Not itself a disease, amenorrhea reflects a failure in the balance among the hypothalamus, pituitary gland, ovaries, and uterus; tumours, injuries, or diseases of these can lead to amenorrhea. Other causes include systemic diseases, emotional shock, stress, hormone over- or underproduction, anorexia nervosa, absence of ovaries or uterus, pregnancy, lactation, and menopause. Infrequent menstruation or amenorrhea not resulting from organic disease is not harmful.[3]

[2] http://www.merriam-webster.com/dictionary/anorexia%20nerv
[3] http://www.merriam-webster.com/concise/amenorrhea

Definition of BULIMIA:
Bulimia (boo-LEE-me-uh) nervosa, commonly called bulimia, is a serious, potentially life-threatening eating disorder. People with bulimia may secretly binge—eating large amounts of food—and then purge, trying to get rid of the extra calories in an unhealthy way. For example, someone with bulimia may force vomiting or do excessive exercise. Sometimes people purge after eating only a small snack or a normal-size meal.

Bulimia can be categorized in two ways:
- **Purging bulimia.** You regularly self-induce vomiting or misuse laxatives, diuretics or enemas after bingeing.
- **Non-purging bulimia.** You use other methods to rid yourself of calories and prevent weight gain, such as fasting, strict dieting or excessive exercise.

However, these behaviors often overlap, and the attempt to rid yourself of extra calories is usually referred to as purging, no matter what the method. If you have bulimia, you're probably preoccupied with your weight and body shape, and may judge yourself severely and harshly for your self-perceived flaws. Because it's related to self-image—and not just about food—bulimia can be difficult to overcome.[4]

[4]http://www.mayoclinic.org/diseases-conditions/bulimia/basics/definition/con-2003305

Eating Disorders Statistics

General:
Almost 50% of people with eating disorders meet the criteria for depression.
• Only 1 in 10 men and women with eating disorders receive treatment. Only 35% of people that receive treatment for eating disorders get treatment at a specialized facility for eating disorders.
• Up to 24 million people of all ages and genders suffer from an eating disorder (anorexia, bulimia and binge eating disorder) in the U.S.
• Eating disorders have the highest mortality rate of any mental illness.

Students:
• 91% of women surveyed on a college campus had attempted to control their weight through dieting. 22% dieted "often" or "always."
• 86% report onset of eating disorder by age 20; 43% report onset between ages of 16 and 20.
• Anorexia is the third most common chronic illness among adolescents.
• 95% of those who have eating disorders are between the ages of 12 and 25.
• 25% of college-aged women engage in bingeing and purging as a weight-management technique.
• The mortality rate associated with anorexia nervosa is 12 times higher than the death rate associated with all causes of death for females 15-24 years old.
• Over one-half of teenage girls and nearly one-third of teenage boys use unhealthy weight control behaviors such as skipping meals, fasting, smoking cigarettes, vomiting, and taking laxatives.
• In a survey of 185 female students on a college campus, 58% felt pressure to be a certain weight,

and of the 83% that dieted for weight loss, 44% were of normal weight.

Men:
• An estimated 10-15% of people with anorexia or bulimia are male.
• Men are less likely to seek treatment for eating disorders because of the perception that they are "woman's diseases."
• Among gay men, nearly 14% appeared to suffer from bulimia and over 20% appeared to be anorexic.

Media, Perception, Dieting:
• 95% of all dieters will regain their lost weight within 5 years.
• 35% of "normal dieters" progress to pathological dieting. Of those, 20-25% progress to partial or full-syndrome eating disorders.
• The body type portrayed in advertising as the ideal is possessed naturally by only 5% of American females.
• 47% of girls in 5th-12th grade reported wanting to lose weight because of magazine pictures.
• 69% of girls in 5th-12th grade reported that magazine pictures influenced their idea of a perfect body shape.
• 42% of 1st-3rd grade girls want to be thinner (Collins, 1991).
• 81% of 10 year olds are afraid of being fat (Mellin et al., 1991).

Collins, M.E. (1991). Body figure perceptions and preferences among pre-adolescent children. International Journal of Eating Disorders, 199-208.

Mellin, L., McNutt, S., Hu, Y., Schreiber, G.B., Crawford, P., & Obarzanek, E. (1991). A longitudinal study of the dietary practices of black and white girls 9 and 10 years old at enrollment: The NHLBI growth and health study. Journal of Adolescent Health, 23-37.

For Women:
• Women are much more likely than men to develop an eating disorder. Only an estimated 5 to 15 percent of people with anorexia or bulimia are male.
• An estimated 0.5 to 3.7 percent of women suffer from anorexia nervosa in their lifetime. Research suggests that about 1 percent of female adolescents have anorexia.
• An estimated 1.1 to 4.2 percent of women have bulimia nervosa in their lifetime.
• An estimated 2 to 5 percent of Americans experience binge-eating disorder in a 6-month period.
• About 50 percent of people who have had anorexia develop bulimia or bulimic patterns.
• 20% of people suffering from anorexia will prematurely die from complications related to their eating disorder, including suicide and heart problems.

Mortality Rates:
Although eating disorders have the highest mortality rate of any mental disorder, the mortality rates reported on those who suffer from eating disorders can vary considerably between studies and sources. Part of the reason why there is a large variance in the reported number of deaths caused by eating disorders is because those who suffer from an eating disorder may ultimately die of heart failure, organ failure, malnutrition or suicide. Often, the medical complications of death are reported instead

of the eating disorder that compromised a person's health.

According to a study done by colleagues at the *American Journal of Psychiatry* (2009), crude mortality rates were:
- 4% for anorexia nervosa

- 3.9% for bulimia nervosa

- 5.2% for eating disorder not otherwise specified

Crow, S.J., Peterson, C.B., Swanson, S.A., Raymond, N.C., Specker, S., Eckert, E.D., Mitchell, J.E. (2009) Increased mortality in bulimia nervosa and other eating disorders. *American Journal of Psychiatry* 166, 1342-1346.

Athletes:
- Risk Factors: In judged sports – sports that score participants – prevalence of eating disorders is 13% (compared with 3% in refereed sports).
- Significantly higher rates of eating disorders found in elite athletes (20%), than in a female control group (9%).
- Female athletes in aesthetic sports (e.g. gymnastics, ballet, figure skating) found to be at the highest risk for eating disorders.
- A comparison of the psychological profiles of athletes and those with anorexia found these factors in common: perfectionism, high self-expectations, competitiveness, hyperactivity, repetitive exercise routines, compulsiveness, drive, tendency toward depression, body image distortion, pre-occupation with dieting and weight.21[5]

[5]ANAD: National Association of Anorexia Nervosa and Associated Disorders

PART ONE

My Story

Chapter 1

"Why do you think having control over everything, this need to have everything the same— why do you think it's so important?"
"Because if things aren't in place, I feel as if I'm falling off a cliff."

Jeff and Jackie Rand

It was in November, 2012, three days after Thanksgiving, when my brother Jeff came by to collect me from Rhode Island Hospital and take me to Johns Hopkins in Baltimore. I was slowly dying from Anorexia, and no one had been able to help me. Rhode Island Hospital wasn't equipped to deal with someone in my condition, even though they'd been doing their level best to keep me alive until a more effective recovery program could be found. But I'd used up all my psychiatric insurance, and the sad fact was no one wanted me because of my condition, age and history. We went to Johns Hopkins because it was the first place that became available. It was also to be my last chance at recovery.

There's not much I remember of that trip to Baltimore, but what I do remember is embarrassing to me now. An unreal image of Jeff suggesting lunch at the airport, but I was completely unable to make such a decision. We agonized over the choices and possibilities until finally deciding on a tuna salad sandwich. Once on the airplane I began eating like the starving person I was. Yet, I only ate half of it (I always eat just half of a sandwich). I also ate an apple. My entire being was soon overcome by a sense of panic, and I became hysterical, crying and saying over and over and over that I shouldn't have eaten so much. Jeff was not only embarrassed, he didn't have any idea how to help me. At one point I even began trying to climb out of my airplane seat and onto his lap—I was feeling that sensation of falling off a cliff, and I wanted to be safe.

I was vaguely aware people were watching me, but I didn't care. In desperation, Jeff asked me if I knew we were on an airplane and could be escorted off because of my behavior. He pulled out his IPod, putting the earphones on my head, with me saying, "Could I please listen to Elton John's *Funeral for a Friend*?" I felt it was quite appropriate for the circumstances.

Listening to the music, I clenched the sides of the chair like the plane had exploded and I was falling through the air. I kept asking Jeff, "How much have I eaten?" And I returned, time and again, to peer inside the bag to find proof of what I'd consumed. I just wanted reassurance, but the problem was inside me. There was nothing he could do.

When the plane finally landed, I remember Jeff scurrying through the airport so fast that I had great difficulty keeping up to him. I kept thinking I shouldn't have eaten the sandwich, repeatedly asking him, "What do I do about the sandwich? I shouldn't have eaten the sandwich. I should never, never, never have eaten that sandwich. Why did you let me eat it? Why didn't you stop me?" and saying, "Jeff, Jeff, Jeff," until he held up his finger and shushed me.

It was throughout this nightmare that my poor brother was renting a car. Once we were in the car and Jeff had turned on the radio, I began daydreaming about Johns Hopkins, about how this famous hospital would even surpass the caring, professional treatment I'd received at UCLA and that someone would finally help me and that I would be safe there.

Baltimore neighborhood near Johns Hopkins

We had difficulty finding Johns Hopkins. The drive took us through an apocalyptic, city jungle that

17

looked like a bombed out war zone. We found
ourselves in neighbourhoods where we received
open mouth stares, as we were the only white people
visible. I was terrified, even though there were cops
on virtually every street corner. Jeff was sweating
and saying, "Fuck, where are we?" He was even too
frightened to ask the cops for help. And I remember
thinking how could Johns Hopkins exist in a place
like this? Little did I know that one day soon I would
be walking these streets myself.

http://www.hopkinsmedicine.org/

When we finally found it, the hospital stuck
out like a huge monstrosity. The parking lot was
across the freeway from the hospital, so we walked
through a tunnel bridge to get there. Jeff asked for
directions and the admissions officer escorted us to
Four North, the same wing I'd stayed on while at
UCLA and, strangely enough, while at Rhode Island
Hospital.

We were seated in the main waiting room
where I saw all sorts of people, not just those with

eating disorders. Eventually a young intern brought us into a small office. She smiled and nodded to me (as I continued to babble on about the tuna sandwich debacle). She asked Jeff and I questions for about half an hour then left.

It wasn't long before a woman who could only be described as a walking battleship came in. Her name was Dr. Margaret Seide. I would have been frightened by her demeanor, but it was getting late, so my focus had now shifted to my normal routine.

"It's five pm," I said. "Where's my dinner?"

Jeff and I have a joke. At five o'clock Rainman watches Jeopardy and at five o'clock Eileen has dinner. That's just the way it is. However, I was told that dinner was at five-thirty and that a nurse would select my food for me. Hearing this, I panicked, telling her exactly what I would require: a salad, a protein, a starch, a veggie and a dessert. This was my blanket. I had to have it. Dr. Seide looked at me incredulously, like she couldn't believe what she was hearing. I soon found out why. When the nurse brought me my dinner there was a tiny piece of fish, some rice and a helping of soggy, green beans.

I pleaded with them, "Please don't go. I need to have a salad and a dessert. I can't eat without having the salad first. This is the way it has always been done. I need to have it. I don't understand." I looked at Jeff and then at Dr. Seide. Jeff turned away, and she said, "Look, what you get is what you get." She watched as I deflated like a balloon in front of her, then she announced, "You aren't in control here. Food selection is a privilege you'll earn, but we'll go into details later." She was pissed because the food obsession was controlling the interview.

Meanwhile I was obsessing about salt, something that occurs when I get seriously underweight. I crave salt, but at the same time I'm terrified to use it. So that's why I want reassurance. I want to feel safe. But as I didn't have the reassurance I was used to getting at UCLA and with my mother, my head was spinning. Again it was that sensation of falling off a cliff, and I had no safety net. I fell, and as I fell I pleaded with Jeff and Dr. Seide, "What do I do with the salt? Is this too much? How much should I use? What should I do with it? What do normal people do?" But all this was beyond the realm of her comprehension, so she said, "That's up to you. You've been given two packets, figure it out."

Except you can't taste anything when your weight gets that low (I was 47 pounds when admitted to Johns Hopkins). It's the result of a zinc deficiency. All your minerals get out of balance when you're in starvation mode. I can recall getting up in the middle of the night and putting salt into the palm of my hand and licking it, because I was craving salt. At the same time I was worrying about it causing constipation. It's enough to drive anyone crazy.

I then began telling the doctor about my usual routine, which included the meal plan I'd used at UCLA, and how I got up every morning at four am to drink coffee because of my bowel obsession. She sat at her desk across from me, shaking her head. The conversation was done.

But I kept on trying. "I can't taste anything," I said. "I need your help! I'm afraid that if I don't use enough salt, I won't digest my meal properly and that if I use too much salt, I'll get constipated. So what's the right amount?" And I kept going on like this, from one vein to another to another, saying whatever thought entered my mind.

When my food was finally done, I explained to her I was very tired and that I often go to bed after eating dinner. I told her my usual bedtime was at seven or eight because I get up so early to try to go to the bathroom. She said, "You'll go to bed at ten. No exceptions."

Instead of what I'd asked for, all 47 pounds of me was told to go sit in the waiting room, where I remained until ten pm when I was finally allowed to go to bed. I was so tired I could barely walk. All I could think about was how well they'd treated me at UCLA, and what in God's name was going on here?

When I was at UCLA, they wanted me to rest. If I couldn't go to bed and I wanted to go lay down, they would have me go to the windowed quiet room across from the nurses desk and curl up on the couch with a pillow—because they didn't want me to be alone and to start stressing about food. At Hopkins all we had was this waiting room where we sat all day, waiting for food, group, rounds and bedtime. If I tried to stand up, the nurses would say that I was attempting to burn calories. It was hellish.

Anyway, when ten o'clock did roll around, I was shocked to be brought into an austere hospital room that was freezing cold. I'd been expecting the kind, gentle, professional care I'd received at UCLA medical center. I assumed Jeff, who was long gone by this time, had no reason to expect anything different. What happened next was nothing like that. They piled cold blankets on top of my wasted body, then used hot water packs to warm me up. I was also put on a heart halter monitor and a pulse oximeter. They awakened me every hour, which wasn't a problem—who could sleep properly with a nurse stationed in the brightly lit, open doorway? The

21

nurse was there because were expecting me to die that night.

At shift change, a feminine looking man came in and took my readings. After speaking with him, I said, "Are you gay?"

I was pissed and was showing it.

He said, "That's not very nice to say."

And I said, "I know you are. I have good gaydar."

He just smiled. Turned out he was a nice guy.

I slept fitfully, and at about six am they took a finger stick. Within minutes, the nurses rushed into my room, one of them looking quite intense. Apparently, my blood sugar had dropped into the 40's, and they came armed with orange juice and graham crackers. They demanded that I eat, explaining to me that my blood sugar was dangerously low.

I said, "These are the rules of my disease. I'm not allowed to eat anything until breakfast time. If I do, it will punish me. That's how it works."

One of the nurses responded by saying, "You're going to eat this AND you're going to eat breakfast."

I said, "I can't do it. Don't you understand? It won't let me eat breakfast. If I eat this it will punish me. It will hurt me. I just can't do it."

She said, "Look, if you don't do this, we're going to have to inject you with sugar. You won't like that. Besides, it's a hell of a lot more calories than the graham crackers and orange juice."

So I agreed to eat the food but not without a bargaining chip.

I said, "I'll do this, but can you make sure I have All Bran cereal with walnuts and soya milk and a banana for breakfast?" This was what I'd been

having for my morning meal every day at Rhode
Island Hospital.

"I'm really too scared to try anything else," I
explained.

She said, "I'll see what I can do."

At breakfast time, a nurse told me to get
dressed so that I could be taken to the dining room. I
was also told I wouldn't be able to select my own
meal, that a nurse would select what I would get to
eat and that meals were based on what is known as a
food exchange program. In this system food amounts
are based on prescribed exchanges of food types. For
example, one sugar could be traded for another sugar
so that a dessert could actually be counted as a fruit.
I was on the lowest exchange level due to the danger
of what is known as refeeding syndrome. All I know
is the nurse found some All Bran for me but no fruit.
I rarely saw real fruit there.

Eileen Rand

Chapter 2

Refeeding Syndrome

What is refeeding syndrome?
Refeeding syndrome can occur when a person is recovering from a period of starvation. If a starving person is fed too aggressively, it can cause refeeding syndrome, which is a dangerous and sometimes fatal condition. It's associated with low levels of phosphate, potassium and magnesium in the bloodstream.

National Institute for Clinical Excellence (NICE) Guidelines for Management of Refeeding Syndrome

Patients at risk for refeeding syndrome have ...

ONE or more of the following:
- BMI (Body Mass Index) <+ 16 kg/m^2
- Unintentional weight loss of >15% in the previous 3 to 6 months
- Low levels of potassium, phosphorous or magnesium before refeeding

OR

25

TWO or more of the following:
- BMI <18.5 kg/m^2
- Unintentional weight loss of >10% in the previous 3 to 6 months
- History of alcohol abuse or drugs including insulin, chemotherapy, antacids or diuretics
denverhealth.org

Who gets refeeding syndrome?
Refeeding syndrome is most commonly seen in patients who have anorexia nervosa, chronic alcoholism, cancer, chronic malnutrition, uncontrolled diabetes, or are post-op and/or have not eaten well for several days. Individuals who are obese and have severely restricted calories and/or sudden weight loss are also at risk. Refeeding syndrome can occur in patients who eat orally or in those who depend on tube feeding for their nutrition.

Why does refeeding syndrome occur?
Refeeding syndrome occurs because the body adapts to starvation. Under normal conditions, the body uses carbohydrate from the diet for energy. If no food is available for 24 hours, the body uses energy that is stored in the liver and muscles. After about 3 days, the body adapts again and uses other stored sources of energy. After a few days of starvation, the body becomes used to starvation.

When a person finally begins eating, the body suddenly shifts back to food as its source of energy. During this shift changes occur in the body processes, which result in fluid and electrolyte imbalances and vitamin deficiencies.

What happens when a person has refeeding syndrome?
Individuals with refeeding syndrome are deficient in

26

potassium, magnesium, and phosphorus, and often are deficient in fluid and a vitamin called thiamine. These nutrients are involved in many important body processes.

As a result of nutrient imbalances, patients who are suddenly refed can have serious complications, including:

Heart problems
Breathing problems
Impaired mental status
Seizures
Paralysis
Insulin resistance
Bone problems

Deaths also have occurred that are associated with refeeding syndrome.

Can you prevent refeeding syndrome?

Yes, usually. The key is to identify if a patient is at risk for refeeding syndrome because of poor intake over a period of time. Once a person is identified as at risk, it's necessary to provide food and fluids slowly during the refeeding process. It's dangerous to provide too many calories and too much fluid to a person whose body has adapted to starvation.

What is the right way to nourish a patient with refeeding syndrome?

It's most important for anyone who was starved for several days to resist the urge to eat and drink large amounts of food or liquid. Several small meals and fluids in small quantities are key to renourishing a starving body. For acutely ill or postsurgical patients who are on tube feeding, it's necessary to provide the feeding in small amounts and then gradually increase the amount.

27

To prevent refeeding syndrome, a person should not receive full feeding and hydration for several days after a period of starvation. It's important to carefully monitor blood nutrients, as well as tolerance to food and fluids. A registered dietitian can help determine how much food and fluids to provide to prevent refeeding syndrome.

How do I know if someone is at risk for refeeding syndrome?

If a patient has gone without much food and/or fluid for 3 or more days, the person is possibly at risk for refeeding syndrome. In general, the more severe the malnutrition, the higher the risk for refeeding syndrome.[6]

[6] http://www.nutrition411.com/patient-education-materials/enteral-and-parenteral-nutrition/item/528-refeeding-syndrome/

Chapter 3

The Truck of Terror

Continuing on, I found myself thinking that Johns Hopkins might not be so bad. The nurse had been nice, and the meal had been alright. But then I found out about lunch; still no choices for me. I was being shown that I wasn't in control here. Not at all. In fact, if you asked your nurse for something, you got the opposite. They enjoyed it. I quickly learned not to do that.

I asked, "What we do all day?"

"You sit and wait for rounds, for one thing," came the reply.

In rounds you came before this whole interdisciplinary team. They had complete control over everything. So, of course, I wanted to know how to get food privileges. It turned out I had to eat one hundred percent of the food put in front of me in three quarters of an hour, and I had to get up to an intake of 3,500 calories. My goal weight? Dr. Seide wouldn't tell me, but she did say it was based on Metropolitan Life statistics of women who lived the longest at a certain age and weight. Well, I'd looked that up before, so I knew I would be expected to gain far more than the 85 pound goal set at UCLA. I tried to bargain with her about this, but she said, "No.

There's no bargaining here. It is what it is." I just sat there flabbergasted. And I was terrified, because I knew I wasn't capable of toeing such a stringent line. Not only did I have to eat all this food, but I had to achieve some unspecified weight. Let's just say for now that I came to call the food trolley "the truck of terror."

The Truck of Terror

It would come at lunch, after rounds and after our occupational therapy (This included discussions about issues like self-esteem and the impact of the media on our food and bodies. For example, they taught us about airbrushing, that the ideal body doesn't exist, that we're chasing after something that isn't even real.).

My first lunch there was unusual. The nurses and the CNA''s (Certified Nursing Assistants) put on a late Thanksgiving dinner. But of course they fed me based on the food exchange. So I was given just the basics. I was really disappointed to see there was no pumpkin pie, stuffing or gravy on my plate. Looking around at all the other plates in the room I could see they had the food items missing from my plate. So I asked why.

The dietician came out, and I began to babble about what I needed from her. She said, "You get what you get." Then she told me that even though I was on the lowest level of exchange, every two days, even if I didn't eat everything that was put in front of me, my food allotment/calories would increase. This would go on until I reached 3,500 calories per day. It was more of there's no "Let's make a deal!" here. However, I still failed to accept that I couldn't bargain, and the staff soon came to consider me as a negotiator.

Johns Hopkins rules were all about behavior modification. Be good and we'll give you eating privileges. Don't be good and we'll put you in isolation or worse. We don't care how you feel, we care how you behave.

It was an approach so foreign to me I just couldn't get it. I cried and I screamed to be heard, even though the nurses didn't want to deal with me. Some put earplugs in while I screamed. I wasn't even an animal to them. I had no value.

As my education continued it became clear there was no safety net. You see, depending on which nurse was on duty your food portions would vary. The amount of food you got was even affected by their moods. It was cruel. There was no predictability. There was no love or kindness. I used to feel like I was in some kind of mad scientist's program. The only thing I knew for certain was you definitely didn't want to be at the nurses desk with your food, where isolation or Haldol shots or even physical restraints were possible.

This first night we had a little African nurse for whom a cup of rice was like a half plate. I wouldn't eat. So, of course, they made me sit at the

31

nurse's desk. I still didn't eat. Oh boy, did I find out what came next. They tried to force me to take some Ativan pills. I wouldn't take them. So they called security, which terrified me. They ended up with nine people holding me down while a nurse pulled down my pants and gave me the Ativan by needle.

On my third day at Johns Hopkins I sat down with the ward psychiatrist. I really liked her. We had a rapport. Our conversation centered on my wish to sign out of the hospital. She was very frank, telling me that if I did so and didn't withdraw my request within a few days, then a hearing would take place to determine if I needed to be committed or could be released. I didn't know that since I'd been admitted they'd been telling Jeff they believed I was dying, so they couldn't let me leave. Because of this, when I called him, he wouldn't come and get me. I ended up withdrawing the request.

I hated eating all the food, and I was constipated. I was also used to a better selection of food and making my own healthy choices. But here I was expected to eat, for example, a plate full of pancakes and syrup; a whole bowl of scrambled eggs plus bacon; a bowl of frosted flakes plus orange juice, yogurt and milk. That was breakfast. They took my blood sugar one morning and it was 220.

Eating the amount and type of food I was expected to consume would often leave me hysterical, so they would give me Ativan to calm me down. The same had worked for me in the Rhode Island Hospital. Johns Hopkins didn't know this or they probably would have realized I was going through Ativan withdrawal.

I continued to refuse to eat, or I ate only under duress, which resulted in the staff setting me up with a sugar IV and an electrolyte IV. They still expected me to eat, though. Not knowing what else to do I put in my second request to leave and didn't rescind it.

So, in early December they had the commitment hearing after all. Jeff, my doctor, a lawyer who had been provided for me, the judge and myself were all in this little onsite courtroom. The doctor stated her piece. I stumbled through my speech. And so it went. At the end of the meeting, I was told by the judge that since I presented a danger to myself I was being committed until the doctors deemed it was okay for me to go. They expected that would be when I'd gained more than 50 pounds over my current weight. I had visions of being put away forever.

I begged Jeff not to leave me there. I felt safe when I was with Jeff and so lonely when he left. He said, "It'll be okay, Leenie." That was his nickname for me.

But I couldn't get through the food, and I became so hysterical they began injecting me with Haldol, which has the side effects of weight gain and constipation—something I already had. But you're in a straightjacket, drooling away. No one listens. And even though my body wanted to move (the drug seemed to make my legs restless) it couldn't. This made the constipation worse.

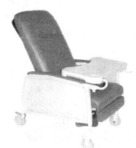

Geriatrics Chair

I began to fight them off when they came with the needle. At first they put me in isolation and strapped me into a Geriatrics chair, where I could scream and scream and scream and nobody heard me. And I was so cold, it felt like being in the Atlantic Ocean with no clothes on.

If that didn't work, I was put into four point restraints in my room for up to six hours at a time and, again, I would scream and cry. But the staff didn't care. I could hear them complaining about being assigned to be my guard—because that's what they were, guards.

Four Point Restraints

The reason they put me on Haldol was because they thought I wanted the Ativan (again, it wasn't a matter of wanting the drug, it was that it kept me from having withdrawal symptoms). However, they soon found out I hated Haldol. I hated the drug so much I would rather have been bitten by a rattlesnake. It was because the two side effects I mentioned earlier were the things I feared most in life. So, of course, it was Haldol for me.

They still had a nurse with me 24/7, even though I was already gaining weight (because I was being force fed and because I was constipated). It was my idea of hell. It got so bad I tried digging the shit out with a pen. All that did was make sure I wasn't allowed pens in the future. Thank the Lord someone eventually believed me when I said I was constipated, and they took care of the problem.

When I finally reached the 3,500 calorie diet, and maintained that level of food intake for a week, I was allowed to pick my food. It was surreal. Going into detail is superfluous and, besides, it didn't make sense other than it was all about fat, starch and sugar intake.

My gums were now bleeding because of all the sugar. We were only allowed to brush our teeth in the morning and at night. It had something to do with the OCD (Obsessive Compulsive Disorder) part of the disease. They said it was an anorexic ritual, that many anorexics will brush their teeth after eating, so that they can't taste the food, thus allowing them to pretend they didn't eat anything.

In addition to the above, my blood pressure and my blood sugar were way too high, but nothing was done about it. I wasn't even allowed to shower or go to the bathroom by myself.

Toward the end of my stay, the new, red-haired doctor made a bargain with me. I don't remember what his end of the bargain was, but I had to take in 4,000 calories. This meant an extra ensure and a packet of cookies before bed. Now, by the end of the day my stomach felt like it was going to burst, but I still had to have that one more ensure. It was horrific. And they still wouldn't give me things to help me have a bowel movement. Only when a much needed x-ray showed constipation did my doctor give me MiraLAX. It worked, but eventually Dr. Seide came back on rounds. She said, "There's no sunshine or rainbows for you," and reduced my MiraLAX intake to every second day. No one argued with her.

The other patients, who were mostly young and inexperienced, were frightened of me. I think I also irritated them. But I really didn't care anymore. Jeff would avoid my calls and when we did talk he was impatient. I was also forbidden to talk to mom. Everything became a blur. I never knew such stark hopelessness. I wasn't allowed out of bed at night, and I was forced to sit all day. They didn't want me burning off calories.

After dinner, as previously mentioned, I thought my stomach was going to burst. I couldn't sleep at night because the lights were on, and I had horrible, horrible indigestion and acid reflux. I was allowed no exercise, no salads, no real fruit. It was hell on earth.

My assigned social worker was not my friend, yet later on during my stay Jeff told me that when I first arrived she went home and prayed for me each night, because everyone thought I was going to die. I was actually shocked that she would care, she certainly didn't show it, and I never felt safe with her.

Many of the staff members were callous. They had me pegged as a manipulator and told Jeff the same thing. Their goal was to bring me to what they considered an ideal weight of about 107 pounds. That was a gain of 60 pounds from when I arrived there. At UCLA 85 pounds maintained was acceptable.

It took a long time, but I eventually achieved one hundred and eight pounds in early April. I was very unhappy with that weight. In fact I was close to being suicidal. I hated my body. I was so uncomfortable that I kept saying this is not me. This is your body not mine. I want my own body back. The worse they treated me the crazier I acted.

36

There were good people there, too, but mostly it was like being in an upside-down Nazi concentration camp. Instead of starving me to death, they were stuffing me to death. And I wasn't the only one with this problem. There was a boy who threw up every time he ate. This would sometimes happen right at the table. They accused him of doing it on purpose and put him in isolation. But he wasn't alone. Others would throw up at the table, and the nurse would just bring over the trash can. We all had to remain where we were. There was something sick and very wrong there. It was so bizarre and unnatural. It couldn't be real. But it was.

The other problem was a sense of reversed prejudice. Many of the staff were local black girls—poor, uneducated and angry. They considered me "The crazy white bitch." They enjoyed calling me that. I remember when I first came there, one black woman came up to me, stuck her finger in my face and said, "You gonna be here a long time white girl." Even Dr. Seide didn't like me. She was often harsh, intimidating and at one point frightened me when she slammed her fist down on her desk while talking to me.

So, with all that said, here's the "Johns Hopkins problem" as I see it: While Johns Hopkins is known for its excellence, it exists as an island in a sea of underprivileged, uneducated people, in a wasteland in what resembles a war-torn ghetto that gives life to the phrase "Concrete Jungle," except this jungle is a jungle of twisted metal and twisted people who work for the 80 building medical campus as janitors, in food service and even as caretakers. The complex has over 80 entrances and receives 80,000 visitors weekly. It houses over 1,000 beds and has a staff in excess of 1,700 doctors with

about 30,000 total employees.[7] This is a huge,
bustling business. It has no time or patience
for someone with the needs I had at the time.

As I mentioned at the beginning of the book
recovery demands that you never be forced or
threatened. Hopkins wasn't interested in recovery.
Their single-minded goal was to increase my weight.

[7]Data taken from Wikepedia article on Johns Hopkins

Chapter 4

The point of this book can be found in 1st Corinthians: Chapter 13. Love, unconditional love, a love that's not worried about 2nd or 3rd or 70th chances and that produces healing–that's what this book is about. Yelling, accusation and punishment only serve to fuel the anorexia. You may teach people to lie better, but you aren't going to cure them.

Statue of Jesus at Johns Hopkins

I want you to understand, specifically, what it
was about my situation that made my illness worse
instead of better. It will also give you further insight
into why programs like the one I was in at Johns
Hopkins don't work.

The first thing I remember at Johns Hopkins
was the cold. Even in my room there was no heat
and, as mentioned, the attendants had to apply hot
packs to keep me warm. The next problem I had was
twofold: I was too weak to move and, even if I could
have moved around, it was forbidden. How do you
stay warm when you can't move?

Then came the forced feedings: I was
expected to eat all meals plus two Ensures (a meal
replacement product) per day, or I would have to sit
in front of the nursing station until I did eat what
was given to me. Of course it was usually the
nursing station for me; I cried all day, every day. I'm
five feet tall and weighed 47 pounds at the time—it
was physically impossible for me to eat the 3,500
calories per day I was expected to consume. And
instead of trying to work through things with me, my
caretakers relied on punishment: being put into
isolation; being buckled into a geriatrics chair; being
given Haldol shots and then put in a straightjacket;
or the worst, being put in four point bed restraints.
Where was the caring there?

Another thing I remember was the callousness
of the staff. None of them were gentle. I suffered
broken and bleeding skin due to my time in
restraints (I had no fat beneath my skin, so my flesh
tore and bruised easily). The nurses were
unnecessarily rough when giving me shots and they
also ripped off my skin when removing the tape that
held the IV's in place. And, of course, they ignored
my pleas and crying and eventual screaming because
of the incredible pain they were causing. Even the

terrible constipation I suffered was ignored. No one showed they cared. To the doctors and the nurses I was an obstacle to a goal they intended to achieve.

Under this horrible regime, I gained about five lbs per week. Our nurse told me it wasn't uncommon for the girls to gain ten pounds per week. At UCLA my dietician told me the exact opposite, that gaining weight too quickly isn't healthy and, besides, making someone who's terrified of gaining weight put on so much in so little time could be psychologically damaging. So, yes, these people were achieving their physical goal, but it was so aversive it created more resistance than it did a will to live.

Even something as simple as food delivery was looked upon as the delivery of terror. Fear was a major factor in most interactions with the staff. My body, my mind and my soul were constantly braced for the next blow. And the excessive food was making me ill.

Since I looked at the staff as jailers, I tried to escape. I called for help. I tried Jeff. I tried my Dementia stricken mother. I tried other relatives. Most had been told ignore these pleadings, to keep conversations brief or to simply ignore them. And since I was caught between the devil and the deep blue sea, I felt I'd nothing to lose. I put in a second request to be discharged.

The founder of the John Hopkins Eating Disorder Program, Dr. Karin Neufeld, was responsible for initiating my commitment hearing. She was successful in her attempt to lock me up, and I was terrified.

I continued to have my own personal sitter. The doctors in rounds were in control of my behavior. There were no choices afforded me (other than the crying and the screaming). I was expected

41

to do what they said. I saw no end. I felt no trust. And the rules continued to change depending on the doctors' moods and what they'd heard from the nurses. There was also the fact that the doctors and the interns on the team were constantly changing. Even the patients came and went. But I stayed. And though I continued to gain weight, nothing was being done to make me well.

Four months later I'd achieved the doctors' desired weight. I'd gone, kicking and screaming all the way. The other patients were afraid of me, they didn't want to be associated with me due to the disdain in which the staff held me and most of them weren't in any condition to understand what was going on. I wasn't only at a point where I felt completely unsupported, I believed I had nothing to lose. Whether the doctors understood it or not, my illness (not so hidden anymore) was in full control.

As I approached my target weight, I was given a choice by the male doctor who was on staff at the time. He said, "Eileen, you like making deals. Here's one for you… If you can do 4,000 calories for a week, I'll let you go into the step-down program." This was a get out of jail free card for me, so of course, I went for it. Anything—I would have done anything to get out. I happily signed the step-down contract, but I knew in my heart it was a contract doomed to fail.

First of all, the crap they were feeding me had pushed my blood sugar into the 200s. My blood pressure, following suit, went as high as 198 over 120. My gums were still bleeding. I was pale and bloated and hated the way I looked. I hadn't even had my hair done in eight months. And my emotions? They were so out of kilter, I was swirling in a kind of maelstrom.

The outpatient program … I was still forced to stay up until ten pm. It was great, though, to sleep in a real bed after all those months in a hospital bed. The other girls had a lot more freedom, because they were compliant. They could come and go as they pleased, even staying out over night, or going to jobs—just having to show up for certain meals and group meetings. The closer they got to discharge, the longer they could stay away.

When I asked the nurses how long I'd have to be in this program, they said I'd be there for at least a month, that they were going to try and teach me how to live—you know, take me shopping, get me cooking and that kind of thing.

The other girls had achieved their own weights and kept them up. My own weight kept yo-yoing, so they would bump up my calories and I'd gain weight, which would end up with my personal demon (the disease) not letting me eat again. It was a vicious ride they did nothing about.

The portioning on our own was even more difficult than in the hospital, as I at least knew the foods they served up there. Here, the girls would select the menu and we would eat either at the cafeteria or cook our own food at the house. The cafeteria portions were actually larger, but when we cooked at the house, the woman who was in charge of the outpatient program (who was grossly obese herself) was rigid with regard to the generally large food portions.

The food exchange still went on, but it was complicated… The sizes didn't make any sense. The pieces could be a normal size or double the normal size but would count as one choice. So, a piece of bread at the house might be the size of a large hamburger bun, where at the hospital it could be just be half of a muffin.

The main portions were eyeballed, rather than measured out. So, the girls might have two meatballs where I would have to eat five; they might have one cup of pasta where I would be given two. And here I was required to have not one, but two desserts with every meal—to make up for the lack of Ensure.

A typical evening meal might be five meatballs, a plate full of pasta (we had to have one hot meal per day), a quarter cup of cheese on top, a cup of vegetables, a glass of juice or soda, a piece of cake and an ice cream bar. Now that might not seem like a lot to you, but to a 100 pound anorexic, such a meal was anathema.

We would have breakfast at the hospital, either at the cafeteria or at the unit (our old ward). I was required to have something different every day, so I couldn't get used to a certain meal. One day I might have to have a donut the size of one of those cinnamon bun kind of things, two pieces of bread, a yogurt and a bowl of canned fruit. And then I'd have to have an omelette. And then I'd have to have some bacon. And then I'd have to have some juice. And, maybe, a cup of cereal.

Lunch would be a tuna salad sandwich or an entire baguette and God knows what was on it, followed by vegetables, milk and juice. And, again, dessert: a bowl of ice cream, or a deli style cookie, and some potato chips and even a candy bar. Large portions for everything.

They were trying to get me used to large meals, but there was no way that was going to work. I used to daydream about not eating. I had heartburn every night and my stomach hurt every day. Constipation still ruled my life. I spent much of my time there crying and complaining about how I felt. I also looked like shit. My face was white and puffy and my hair was thinning. I felt like Baby Huey—

this big fat duck running around in diapers and crying. I felt so ugly and miserable.

I was used to people like my mother or the people at UCLA being somewhat patient, kind and responsive to my obvious distress. But this staff was incapable of any kindness or tolerance. They simply weren't interested in my feelings, a point they reminded me of time and time again. Even the other residents had no tolerance for my tears and distress. I suppose they were all in their own private hells, doing what they could to toe the line and get out of there.

I wasn't doing well, and I wanted to go home, but home no longer existed for me. In fact I remember one conversation I had with Jeff. I was crying and begging, "Please, I just want to go home." Jeff's response was, "You don't have a home." It was traumatic and left me desperate. To make matters even worse, I once heard his wife, Jackie, yelling in the background. Then she got on the phone and said, "You're a big baby. Why don't you leave us alone." Then she said, "If anything happens to my husband—if he has a heart attack—it will be your fault, and I'll never forgive you."

Words like this were blow after blow. I felt my face was black and blue, like a prize fighter. Everything had been taken from me—my body, my home, my family. Even Jeff's wife said, "We hate you, and no one cares." But in spite of all this, Jeff still wanted me to have a life.

In the meantime people at the hospital had grown weary of the constant struggle between me and their program. It seemed I was incapable of following their rules. I was told that further noncompliance would result in my dismissal and that Jeff wouldn't take me back. I was obviously incapable of hearing any wake-up calls, because I soon breached the contract. They said, "That's it. You're done."

They gave me a list of homeless shelters and told me I could come back the next day and be re-admitted to the home, but I had to be 100 percent compliant from then on. I packed my bags, and I was to be escorted by security off the property. But when we got outside, I realized I'd forgotten the list of shelters, so I asked to be allowed back in to get them. They told me to keep right on walking off Johns Hopkins property. I was terrified.

I was looking down these bleak streets surrounding this state of the art hospital. It was like I'd fallen out of the sky into this burned out, bombed, hell hole. It looked like Germany must have looked like after World War II. You wouldn't believe the urban blight, the dilapidated buildings.

I kept trying to get back, thinking, "They can't do this to me."

But they could, and they did. The security men grabbed me by the shoulders and pushed me into the street. Then they took my bag, throwing it out into the street as well, saying, "Get off Johns Hopkins property."

I didn't know what to do. I began asking for help. But people just kept looking at me. People were heartless; Jeff was heartless. He was cold. He had no idea. I'm amazed I can forgive him for anything. It's crazy when the person who is caring for you and who says he love you takes the hospital's word over yours. And if he did that once who's to say he won't do it again? This is why I get terrified of Joanne (Cortland's administrator) weighing me.

She'll say to Jeff, "Your sister's not being compliant. What are we going to do with your sister?" I'm terrified it's going to happen again (living on the street). I don't trust him. I don't trust Jeff. I don't trust anyone. Why should I?

Anyway, they'd given me some bus tokens, and I was trying to find the street for the one home I remembered. When I asked a bus driver for help, she said, "I think I know where it is. I'll take you down close to where you want to go."

The bus was full of black people who kept on staring at me. I was overwrought with emotion. When I got off the bus, I looked around and saw a church. I went over and banged on the door. An old man with scary, blood-shot eyes who was emaciated, had yellowish skin and alcohol on his breath was sitting on the steps beside me. A woman finally answered the door.

She said, "Oh honey, that's just down the street. That's the Karis Home."

Eileen Rand

Chapter 5

*For a lot of us, Anorexia becomes like a cleft in
the rocks of that cliff I mentioned. It's the one thing
that's stable when your job's going haywire, and
money is haywire, and families are haywire, because
for every girl you ever talk to their disease will have
certain patterns. Patterns that become like a
familiar, well worn path—they become that cleft in
the rock.*

The Karis Home is the women and children's
division of the Baltimore Rescue Mission. The
ministry was founded back in the 1970s and like the
rest of the Baltimore Rescue Mission the Karis
Home has grown and developed through the years.
Karis actually means Grace when translated from
Greek. And I believe the "Grace Home" was the
place where the seed of my belief in God was
planted.

The Karis Home is in operation to provide
emergency short-term help for homeless women and
children. Guests check in each day around four p.m.
On the top story there's a rectangular room with
about 12 bunk beds. The second floor houses the
chapel and the dining room . Everyone eats their
evening meal at five-thirty pm; the gospel service is
at seven pm. After the service you can take showers

and get ready for bed. Lights are out at nine or ten pm.

Lights are back on at six am. Breakfast is a do-it-yourself thing at seven-thirty and each one of us had a chore we had to do or you'd get kicked out. Everyone had to be gone by eight am. The normal stay for Karis home guests is 30 days.

The Karis Home for Women and Children

I found it, this little shoe-box of a place, next to a closed up building. On the other side, attached to it was the Baltimore Rescue Mission. The air was filled with this awful stench. When I rang the bell next to this meshed, jail-type, barred door, it was opened by a skinny, toothless, old white woman with stringy black hair who smelled of cigarette smoke and looked the epitome of the aged homeless.

When I reminded the woman (her name was Miss Jerry) that I'd called earlier, she informed me they had a bed, but I couldn't be let in prior to four pm. Not knowing the time, I waited helplessly until that hour arrived.

Once inside, a black woman with dreadlocks who went by the name of Miss Suki took me into her care.

"Guess what?" she asked, in a heavy, southern accent. "I'm a gonna get you a bed."

Then, "Guess what? I've got a place to lock up your stuff."

Then, "Guess what …

This continued on until I'd been led to the kitchen—run by the rescue mission—and read the rules. I had to leave at eight am and couldn't return each day until four pm. Dinner was a soup line at five-thirty pm per day. No drugs were allowed.

A little after four pm the women living in this place came filing on in. Some of these people I remember; most I do not. It was a scary time for me.

There was one white woman who was an alcoholic. I remember her, because she got kicked out for drinking.

Then there was Miss Debra. She was a severe crack addict and alcoholic whom they'd rehabilitated. However, through a series of troubles she was back in the home but working during the day at one of the local schools at a cafeteria. She had worked at Karis before as one of the supervisors, so she was kind of up on things. Miss Debra was very nice to me and had a great sense of humour. She could imitate anyone on TV and loved to tell sexually explicit jokes, but she was also a die-hard Christian who would give the bible study in the evening.

Another lady whom I admired very much was at Karis Home even though she had recently held a job at the Mayor's office. You see, her daughter was married to a man who was very violent. He came in one day and shot her daughter and her baby. The poor woman had a breakdown and couldn't function.

51

She had this lovely apartment in downtown Baltimore, but she lost everything, because she didn't care anymore. So after a couple of months of mourning—if you were in a special situation, Karis would sometimes wave their 30 day rule, allowing you to remain for a longer period—she got an entry level position at a lawyer's office. She was now saving her money, and by the time I left she had saved enough to be able to get back into a condo. So, if you were a good risk, Karis Home would let you stay, but if you were just biding your time or waiting for a government check, out you went. In her case they extended her stay for three months, because she was trying to get back on her feet. They also extended my stay.

But even this woman, my friend, turned on me because of the other ladies. It was kind of like a pack mentality. So she was kind to me at first, but then her behavior seemed to change. Part of it was due to staff rotation. Sometimes more good people would rotate in than not. Other times it was hell.

The real problem, I think, was this one woman in the bunk below me—Miss Linda from South Carolina. We had a misunderstanding. It was something stupid. One day I fell asleep while I was reading my Bible. The book tumbled from my hands and landed on her head. She accused me of dropping my Bible on purpose, of attacking her.

I told her, "If I was going to attack you, it certainly wouldn't be with a Bible."

That didn't go over well. She started a campaign against me. She would say things to the other women ... that I was ... well, it was just weird stuff. It was during this time my friend turned away from me. I figured even though she was an educated woman it was the mob mentality that people sometimes seem to arrive at. I don't know what Miss

52

Linda told her but it must have been something significant.

Anyway, I stayed the first evening there. In the morning Miss Jerry made this rich, black coffee (I love my coffee). I was able to enjoy two big cups as well as the relief of being able to go to the bathroom after suffering from constipation for so long. Then, since I was supposed to be back to Johns Hopkins for reassessment at eight am, I decided to go—against the advice of Miss Jerry.

She was right. It wasn't long before the halfway house kicked me out for good. It started on a weekend when I tried to take a Caesar salad at dinner. This wasn't one of the food choices I was allowed to make, and when I brought my food back to the unit, the nurse on charge took it away. My dinner was replaced with something else when the food cart came up. On Monday I was put before the board, but they decided to let me have a week to see what happened. Except I kept having breakdowns. Then, on the following Sunday, I was given a Mexican salad just loaded with beans and meat and cheese and sour cream and guacamole—enough to feed three people—plus a soda and two desserts. I had to bring it from the cafeteria up to the hospital unit and eat it in front of the nurses. I did manage to eat the entire meal, but then I had a meltdown. This meant I sat there until nine-thirty pm, when they let me go back to the house to get ready for bed.

I knew I was in trouble, so I used that half hour before lights out to I call everyone I could think of who might take me in. Jeff listened to what I had to say, then he said, "You were told these things were going to happen. Have a nice life," and he hung up.

The next morning during rounds Dr. Karin Neufeld remarked that she had heard how I'd

53

conducted myself. Then she said, "You're behavior is atrocious. You're disrupting the unit, and you'll have to go. We'll allow you to call the Karis home, but your brother will not take you back."

I had this incredible sinking feeling and I said, "Please give me another chance."

She said, "No. You've been here for five months. You've made it miserable for us and yourself. We've done all we can do. Your brother has done everything he can do. This is it. You're done."

When I called Jeff he said, "You've done this to yourself. You chose this. You chose it."

So they allowed me to call the mission, and I talked to Miss Jerry, who made it possible for me to come back. One of the women from the house and a security guard walked me to the house from the unit and watched me pack my things. The whole time the woman was taunting me saying, "How could you behave like that?" and "You're getting what you deserve," and "Nobody here likes you," and "You won't make it on the street," and "You won't survive."

But I was lucky for the first time in a long time—not only did the mission take me back, I was allowed to stay for a month.

A black pastor ran the mission. Miss Janna and her husband owned the mission, but the pastor ran it for them—both the women's side and the men's side. He told me Johns Hopkins was an experimental hospital and no good for people like me. This is why I was given a month to find another place to live.

Jerry was nice. I felt safe around her. Suki was nice as well. She was nice, but she scared the hell out of me. Miss Jerry was my go-to person. She became more and more beautiful as I got to know her. I even began to see her as an older, wise Indian woman (She was, in fact, part Indian)

Everyone went to Miss Jerry for help, and it ended up breaking her heart, because she knew what went on up in the bunkhouse—the child abuse—but she couldn't do anything unless she caught them in the act. And these people were very clever about their activities. What happened to many of those kids really upset her. She was fierce when it came to protecting the children. Otherwise she was so incredibly gentle. So gentle, in fact, that many people tried to take advantage of her. She often ended up with extra chores, but she never complained.

One bright spot in my own day was the good, strong coffee Miss Jerry made every morning. There was also this day shelter run by a downtown church. It was called My Sister's Place. You were picked up by bus in the morning. When you arrived, they would serve you breakfast, then you would spend the day in a sitting room. There were some things to help pass the time, and you could do your laundry there. They even served lunch and they took you back to your shelter at night.

The relief was short-lived, though, as within a few days I stopped feeling safe at My Sister's Place. I found two women having sex in the bathroom. They got mad at me. Threatened me. Plus there were transvestites using the same washroom as the women.

One black guy dressed up like Shirley Temple. He had a cart in which he carried his make-up. It sported a model head that had its own orange, curlicue wig. The fellow said he was studying to be a beautician. Sometimes he talked like a woman and sometimes he didn't. He definitely looked more like a guy, but he was still very pretty.

My Sister's Place (on the right)

He and another transvestite would usually fight at lunch time. Perhaps one would get more tuna on his sandwich than the other. The two would then start slapping each other with their hands. There was a violent schizophrenic who would notice and begin to act out. It was like a domino effect, and it was awful. To get caught in one of those things was terrifying. In fact, one day one of the transvestites pulled a knife. I was sitting right next to him and although he was aiming for the other guy he just about slit my throat. I fell over backwards in my chair.

When I got up, I immediately panicked and left the building. I spent the rest of the day walking in the streets of Baltimore to get home. After that episode Miss Jerry told me to spend my days at the harbour, because that's where all the tourists were. "You'll be safe down there," she said.

So that's what I did. I got up every morning and walked down to the harbour. Talk about a stark contrast! I walked through these housing

developments. Kids doing drugs on the streets. I
walked past this man every day; he lived in a bus
shelter. Many more people lived under a bridge that
was on my way. Occasionally a big man from one of
the churches would come and distribute food down
there. People didn't pay me any attention, though, so
I wasn't scared.

When I reached the harbour, everything was
different. I tried sitting in Whole Foods like I used to
do with my mom. I remembered how she would let
me get whatever I wanted, but now I didn't have any
money at all. So I spent my days sitting in the midst
of this beautiful tourist area just two blocks from
places where drugs were being sold on the street by
people dressed in John Hopkins uniforms and where
others had sex in darkened alleys.

How was I doing otherwise? I wasn't eating. I
wouldn't eat the food unless there was a salad. Most
of the time it was things like fried chicken and mac
'n cheese. Stuff I would never eat on my own. But I
still weighed in at one hundred ten pounds. My
belly was distended (so distended that when I was
showering, one of the ladies asked me if I was
pregnant). I still couldn't go to the bathroom on a
regular basis. And, of course, I kept freaking out. I
didn't recognize myself. I became afraid to eat at the
shelters. And so, finally, I began to lose weight
again.

Throughout this time Miss Jerry was talking
to Jeff. He sent fifty dollars, my ID, my SIN card
and my Driver's license. I figured he was done with
me. But I was still relentless with my calls.

I talked to Miss Jerry about my old life in La
Jolla, a place she couldn't even imagine. I also
talked to Miss Janna, and she was like, "What are
you doing here?"

They saw I was trying. Every night at Chapel, I was accepting Jesus into my heart (because as a Christian you have to accept Jesus, as he is the only one who can save you from the wrath of God). The minister kept telling me I only had to do it once, but I wanted to make sure I got it right, that it was like having insurance. You know, I'm so foolish, and I've messed up all my relationships, but the more I read the Bible the more I understand that God loves people like me. That's when his power shows up the greatest. He takes the foolish things in the world to confound the wise. And that's what I like. I think if he can do anything for me, then he can do anything for anyone.

And maybe he did do something for me, because the people running the home began calling Jeff in earnest, and little by little they convinced him to take me back.

I also kept calling Jeff. But he was very angry. John Hopkins had told him that if he rescued me, he'd just be repeating the pattern, so just let me fall; let me hit bottom. It was Greg and Jeff's old wash, rinse, repeat cycle. I didn't know that. I'll never know what he thought, because Jeff doesn't talk to me. I'll never know if he intended to find me a place or if he planned to leave me at the shelter. Because he finally did find one. It was Cortland Place, a senior assisted living home back in Rhode Island.

I was let into Cortland as an exception. It was for several reasons, because to get into a place like that you normally have to be 55 years or over. First, they take people with physical handicaps—which I do have. Then I have these problems due to mental disease. And, of course, we were able to pay. I was accepted despite my history at various hospitals and my history of non-compliance: the administrator said, "We'll give it a shot."

cortlandplace.com

It was the beginning of May when Jeff and Jackie found Cortland Place. They said they would pay for it and help me get set up, but I was told that I was not ever going to live with them and that if I screwed up here, that would be it. They would be done.

Jeff sent me cab fare to the airport for May sixth, 2013. Unfortunately, I'd taken my clothes to My Sister's Place and had left them there to be washed. When I went back, they were all stolen. I told Miss Jerry, who knew I was down to 85 pounds, so she took me to the children's closet. The only thing that fit me made me feel like I was wearing a sailor's suit. Then, when I went to get my hair done at the barber shop, there were two very large black men there. I felt scared to leave. One of them said, "Sit down." I could immediately tell the man wasn't cutting my hair properly, but when I said something, the look he gave me scared me to death. He said, "I know what I'm doing." He didn't, though, and I ended with a 1980s, David Bowie haircut. Miss Jerry tried to help me fix it, but we ended up just cutting it really short. I was a mess.

Miss Jerry also made the trip to the airport with me, because I was scared to go by myself. She was such a lovely lady. I forgot about getting her home, though, and I had to rush around to find a machine where I could get some cash to pay her way back. She was great.

Unfortunately Miss Jerry has an addict son who lives on the Men's Side of the Mission. He constantly takes money or she gives him money. He promises to give it back, but he never does. I bought her cigarettes whenever I could, because she'd have given him all the money she had.

We still write to each other. I also call her. She's truly selfless.

Jeff picked me up at the airport. He took me to Panera for my first real food. It was a bowl of black bean soup. Then he took me to get my hair fixed and on to Cortland Place. I couldn't believe it. I was in shock—like going from Kansas to Oz.

I met Joanne the administrator and Jen the admissions officer. Jen is this beautiful young girl in her twenties, just full of life. She showed me my room. Jen also washed the t-shirts and nightgown I had managed to collect at the home.

That night I went to the dining room, but I didn't eat because it didn't feel "safe."

On Monday I was able to buy clothes and food so that I could make a dinner I was comfortable with. I also managed to get a full sized fridge and a stove for my room. I was losing weight though, so they encouraged me to go back to the dining room. It was a battle.

ભ

Somewhere in July or August the idea was fielded that I might return to Atlanta where my ailing mother was (she had Dementia). When we

60

made it there to check out possible living arrangements for me and got to see mom, she was this hunched over baby bird, completely in her dementia. I sang to her while we were there.

The problem with "the plan" was I'd continued to lose weight. I was now down to seventy pounds. No one in Atlanta wanted to take me on unless my weight began to go up again. So we went back to Rhode Island—Jeff to his home and I to Cortland Place.

Labour Day weekend Greg called us and said we needed to get to Atlanta. Mom was going fast. That's how it came to be that on September fourth I was the last one with mom. I was singing to her and holding her and touching her and talking to her, and I put little stuffed animals all around. A hospice nurse was in the room. I told her, "She's going through customs right now."

She smiled and said, "I know, honey."

I sang *You are my Sunshine* to her. Then I said, "Momma, you don't have to stay. You can go if you want to."

Richard and Elise Rand

About 15 minutes later she was gone. The hospice nurse later told me that mom waited for me, that she wanted me. And I was okay. I thought I'd witnessed something extraordinary. I could almost see the angels coming down to get her.

Jeff and I flew home the next day.

September 13 was the funeral in San Diego. We flew her out there. I had the privilege to pick out what she would wear. As per usual, my sister-in-law and my brother Greg were cruel to me. She made fun of me when I got up to do the Eulogy and during the service itself.

However, I ended up with the title for this book from that funeral. Because when Jeff went up to speak he talked about how soldiers who go out to battle try to have everything done in their life that needs to be done, so that should they die in battle, they'll have left nothing on the field.

When our mother died, she left nothing undone. She left nothing on the field. She did her job. She saw that each of us was okay.

My mother had an innate grace, a sense of dignity and poise. I, on the other hand, am a squiggle in a world full of straight lines. I'm an Etch-a-Sketch™ gone crazy. Yet I've always wondered how I can achieve my mother's grace.

In the Bible it says that God is love. Perhaps he's letting me have time to find my way because he loves me. And I'm trying to learn how not to be a squiggle or, at least, learn how to live with being a squiggle.

If my mother wasn't about love, I'd never have made it to this age, although you'll find others saying that she facilitated my illness, that she made my illness possible, that she kept me from getting well. I don't believe that's true.

I had an anorexic friend who died from this beast at age 22. Her family and friends counseled her mother, Mary, that she be cut off. You know, Mary told me that if she had accepted what everyone was saying to her about Cara, she wouldn't have been able to deal with her feelings. It was only by giving her all to Cara that she could live with the tragedy in her life.

And when I called Mary to tell her about my mom and how things had been going, she said, "Eileen you've got to write a book." That's how Mary came to introduce me to the author who's been working with me on the very book she mentioned.

Eileen Rand

Chapter 6

"From here, we'll go back to when I was a little girl—to where it all began. And not knowing what will happen makes me feel like I'm going to fall off that cliff."

Lonely cliffs, San Diego, California

I lived in a typical, middle class tract home in Southern California in the 1960s. Father was a Navy Jag and then moved into private practice. The town was called Clairmont; father worked for a firm in San Diego. The suburban neighbourhood we lived in had only been constructed in the post war building boom of the 1950s, so the buildings were new and the development was filled with young families with kids.

The youngest of three children, I was born in 1964. Jeff was eight years older and Greg was two years older. As the youngest, I felt safe and cared for. I was a typical kid—creative, playful and joyful. My school was on the terrace above our house. I could see where I lived from the parking lot.

As background: we were north of San Diego and Clairmont now has a population of 80,000. But when I lived there adult life was more like the *Mad Men* on television and children were living the life of *The Sandlot* or *Stand By Me*.

I remember lots of bikes, canyons to play in and ice plants to slide on. These were small cactus-like plants with no sharp edges. Their flowers were purple and they almost looked like an outdoor sea anemone. When squished, water came out of them, and they made for an excellent sliding environment.

Ice Plants

Ice Plants in bloom

I had a perfect mother and father, a perfect home and a perfect life. Except that I had a birthmark on my neck. This didn't fit. Even at age five or six I had a strong sense of my body. So, over time, I became self conscious of the mark and began to wear a choker (Remember those?) to cover it. It was a foreshadowing of where my body consciousness was going to take me.

During this time, my dad was becoming successful. Having come from poverty and knowing his wife (whom he had met on a furlough during the war) hated the early years of their marriage, he was driven to succeed. My mom spoke to me about that time. She remembers when visiting that everyone in the small house his family owned would sleep in one large bed. Her mother-in-law snored; mom would sit up all night and cry. Anyway, when I was between six and seven years-old, some of the partners retired and dad bought out the business.

6730 Muirlands Drive as it is today

Along with his new affluence, dad wanted to move to La Jolla (pronounced La Hoya). It's an Indian name. It means the pit, but locals call it the jewel. You know there's the valley of the dolls? Well, we had this pit.

The house he chose was a beautiful but dilapidated mansion. There was this semi-circular drive and a Eucalyptus tree in the front. The inside was a nightmare. All I can remember was this worn, 1970s style, orange carpet. It was hideous. The backyard had a swimming pool, but it was overgrown—the whole back yard was overgrown.

Eileen in happier times

A fenced off garden within the borders of our property was hard to get to. But when you did, you were met by this jungle. It was just like *The Secret Garden*. Lots of fruit trees and interesting stuff for a kid my age.

The Secret Garden

It was isolated, though. There were no other kids in the neighbourhood. Even though we knew our neighbours, everyone kept to themselves. Over time my parents became preoccupied with fixing the place up. It seemed like we lived with the decorators. And since we'd moved in June, there wasn't even school to keep me occupied. The boys had their bikes (they were 13 and 9 at the time) and cub scouts and the beach. I was put in front of the TV every day. I was very lonely and would often dream of finding a friend. Sometimes I would go into kitchen and eat. If one Twinkie was good, then more of them must be better, I thought. It wasn't long before I began to get chubby.

Then school came up. I was gawky and unsophisticated, while the other kids were rich kids with everything going for them. They had cool

clothes and haircuts. They knew all the hot rock n'
roll songs. They were all willowy and beautiful. And
they would tease me about my weight. This went on
for half a year, until I was attacked by two boys on
the way home. Mom wouldn't have that, so I was
moved to All Hallows School.

On my first day, the nuns walked me into
third grade. The kids looked at me as if I wasn't
human, as if I was a bug. And I knew enough to fear
them. For the next year and a half I was really and
truly alone. I was under constant attack. I began to
have difficulty sleeping. Anxiety was prevalent.
Symptoms like getting hysterical about little things
began to show. My mother couldn't understand how
scraped feet from sand in the pool could be the cause
of such dramatics.

As the abuse escalated to the physical, I
became terrified to go out on the playground. Mostly
I would sit at the far edge of the baseball field and
play with toys I brought from home. The other
students would take my toys and break them. One
day they asked me to join in their play. If I gave
them all piggyback rides, I could stay and they
would be my friends. But the other children stuck
needles in my behind while I was carrying someone
on my back and, thus, couldn't get away. They also
failed to keep their promise. I felt so stupid.

Enrolled in summer school at a nearby public
school, the abuse was even worse. They called me
Bozo, even though I was very good at schoolwork.
Sometime during that summer, I began to think of
myself as non-human. I was often beaten on the way
home. And the one time I complained, I was berated
by the principal for saying anything, for wasting
both my mother's time and his over a little teasing.
One day going up to the board the class began to
sing the Bozo song and call me names. The

substitute teacher for the day asked me if what the
other children were doing bothered me.

I said, "No, I'm used to it."

He said, "Interesting," and nothing more.

I felt like garbage.

Over the years, my father was distant. I could
tell he was disappointed with his daughter. Mother
was kind, though. Jeff was good to me, as well, but
he had his own life. Greg was just plain and simply
mean. So, with all these negatives in my life, at the
end of the grade six year, I vowed I was going to
change myself over the summer holidays. I
embarked upon a diet to end all diets.

Now, mother cooked a gourmet dinner every
meal. She was a Better Homes and Gardens mom. If
she found a new and exciting recipe, it was sure to
make it to our dinner table. Dinner at six pm, every
night. I would eat small portions of everything—like
my mother who was very careful about maintaining
her figure. I began exercising. I went to the beach
everyday to get tanned. I learned the music of the
time: *ELO, Heart, Led Zeppelin.*

When summer ended, and I switched to
Muirlands Junior High, I found that I was in the
lowest echelon of the school hierarchy, but I wasn't
a leper. I even made a friend named Kirsten. She
was naturally thin. It was kind of fun. We made
friends with a lifeguard at the beach, and he kept an
eye on us as we played in the unique kids pool.

Children's or Seal Cove at La Jolla

A sea wall built in 1931 protects the beach at Seal Cove from crashing waves, making it a favorite spot for divers, swimmers and families with children. Before the "wave wall" was built, there was a shallow water area between a large rock and a mainland bluff called "Seal Rock Point." The sea wall was built on top of several rocks, across the channel. It's topped by a paved walkway protected by railings.

Local philanthropist Ellen Browning Scripps paid for the sea wall project in order to create a Children's Pool, a place where children could play and swim that would be protected from the (sometimes rather large) waves coming onshore. Ms. Scripps gave the completed project to the City of San Diego. The gift was confirmed by an act of the Legislature, signed by the Governor in 1931, which says that "said lands shall be devoted exclusively to public park, bathing pool for children, parkway, highway, playground, and recreational purposes", while specifying that the area should remain available for fishing.

In the more than 70 years since the sea wall was built, roughly three quarters of the pool area within the sea wall has filled up with sand, greatly decreasing the protected area available for recreational swimming.[8]

Anyhow, it was then that my life changed. I got appendicitis. My weight was average going in, but when sick I lost more. Everyone noticed and wanted to know how I got to looking so good. Mom paid attention. Teachers worried. And I came up with the idea that this was the way to have it all (my dreams). That's when weight loss became my identity. It took me over before I knew it. I felt like I was going from being a prisoner in my body to having the key to the prison.

[8]Data taken from Wikepedia article on Sea Cove, La Jolla

Eileen Rand

Chapter 7

"I know the running is killing me."

After my bout of appendicitis, I began to write a book in the style of Black Stallion by Walter Farley. My heroine was named Annie; her horse was named Satin. As I've mentioned, I was always good at schoolwork, and I'd begun writing stories at a very young age. I wrote new installments of my story every week, then my English teacher, "Mr. Ed," whom we all looked up to, would read them to the seventh grade class. It was well received, but rather than making me popular, the story gave me a certain notoriety.

Eileen's Stallion

On other fronts, I began to have periodic
binges as I grew (you can only go without food for
so long when your body's growing)—this would
have been between Junior High and High School,
the summer between ninth and tenth grade. I even
went jogging after my operation, though I'd been
warned against any form of exercise. Oh yes, I ran,
even to the point of ripping out stitches. I was very
much at war with my body. Not only would I
exercise, but I'd take enemas to help purge what I
ate during my binges.

My family didn't have anything to do with
me, so Mom would try to treat me with food, taking
me to a specialty store called Jonathan's and letting
me pick whatever I wanted to eat. She took care of
me and nurtured a protective relationship with me.
But I had to keep secrets, because I knew my
behavior wasn't normal.

As I grew, I began to gain weight, and the
chaos threw my body out of whack. It terrified me
(worse than facing a firing squad). I got my period at
13 but it had stopped by the time I was 15. The
weight gain took me from 90 to 110 pounds. It
mortified me, because I was going into high school,
and I was even more desperate to make it as a
popular kid.

The school was quite cliquish. There were the
poor black kids and Hispanic kids that were bused
into La Jolla. Then there were the rich kids with
their fancy clothes and hair styles and cars. And then
there was me.

I began to live in a fantasy world, being
determined to have what I saw on TV. This was
1980, and I still had no self-confidence. I couldn't
find my balance. Then I learned about Bulimia—the
throwing up worked. I began to lose weight again. I

also discovered diet pills: you could buy Dexatrim over the counter. I lost more weight.

One of the turning points in my life happened when a popular girl asked to come and sleep over. She wanted to see her 21 year-old boyfriend; I was just her cover. He took us to his apartment. We began drinking alcohol that was disguised as fruit punch. It wasn't long before I began to hang all over her boyfriend, which she didn't like. So he called up some friends to keep me busy. But I got so drunk I passed out.

When I woke up at home the following morning, they told me that while I was in this state I was taken advantage of. The girl had laughingly told my parents I'd lost my virginity. It was an awful scene.

My father took me into a side room and slapped me several times, calling me a whore, a slut and no daughter of his. The only way, he said, that I could remain in his house was to work for my room and board. He immediately found a rake, put it in my hands and set me to work in the back yard.

When the mother of the other teen found out what had happened (she was from Sweden and was very liberal), she said it was no big deal, to chill out, and that it was bound to happen at some point.

But there wasn't a chance my mom and dad were going to chill out. I lost my bedroom and was put in an ante room close to the attic. My father also told me if I was pregnant I would have to keep and care for the baby. He didn't know my periods had stopped.

The situation could have quickly become untenable, but there was a tree by my window. I was able to get out when I needed to.

I did some sleuthing, found the guy who'd raped me and began to see him and hang out at the beach with all these lowlifcs. I guess I was trying to legitimize the rape. If he went out with me it meant that he liked me and that made everything okay. I also thought that being sexually active was another way to be popular.

My mom took me to see a psychiatrist who happened to be a pill pusher. She had me on a lot of things: Lithium, Valium, Librium, Dalmane, sleeping pills and other things. Then I began to take amphetamines during the day and alcohol at night. My emotions were totally out of control. I was so out there that when I walked by kids at school they would hum the theme from the twilight zone. My role model was Janis Joplin.

Eventually, I left the beach crowd. By this time I was sick on both a physical and emotional level and was overwhelmed by my eating behaviours. My weight ballooned up to 120 pounds.

There's one event that should be mentioned. I tried to kill myself at age 15. I'd gotten hold of a couple of bottles of sleeping pills. I took them at eight pm, but I was still awake at midnight. It was then I had a terrible vision of hell. I was falling in a tunnel that was so dark and so cold I was more terrified than at any other time in my life. Then I heard God deep within my being, saying "I'm giving you a chance, please take it." So I went downstairs and called 911. They told me to go and tell my parents what had happened. But I must have wakened my father, because he came down and told me to go back to my room. I explained to him what I'd done, but he still told me to go to my room. I said, "I have to go to the hospital." He hung up the phone and pushed me toward the stairs. It wasn't until 911 called us back and told my dad that he had to get me to the hospital that he agreed to do so. He pulled me up the stairs by my hair, threw me into my room and told me to get dressed. My mom came out then, asking what was going on.

He said, "Did you know this idiot just tried to kill herself?" Then he continued, "The only reason I'm taking you to the hospital is I don't want an ambulance showing up in front of this house."

In the car, he taunted me by asking me if I was going to write a poem about the experience. You had to see it to believe it. Dad was like Mr. Rogers with a chainsaw. When we finally got to the hospital, dad took me to the reception desk and said, "She tried to kill herself," then he turned around and left. Mom came in a little later. My stomach had already been pumped.

Next morning a psychiatrist explained that I did it for attention and would be okay. Mom began to try to find any kind of help she could for me. I even took time off from school.

When I returned, my old friend was dating a popular surfer. I met one of his friends who lived on the beach. The problem was that he only wanted sex. He'd heard about me and would bring me to his home in the afternoons, and we would drink and have sex. If his friends dropped by, he told me to hide in the closet. He didn't want them to know he was with me. I wasn't "cool" or attractive enough. He also put me down sometimes, but I said nothing. I felt I deserved it. The whole thing made me feel sick inside.

At home, the guilt and dirty feelings made me think I was human garbage. I didn't care about anything or anybody. But I was too afraid to try and kill myself. The only thing I was doing at the time that could be seen as positive was my writing. In fact, I wrote a book of poetry.

I stopped seeing him when I met another young guy who reminded me of the lead singer of

79

Yes, a group I was really into at the time. I was
playing the hippie queen, doing drugs, smoking and,
of course, running and throwing up. We began to go
out together. We started a band called *Back Door*. I
was the lead singer, and I'd drink before, during and
after our shows. I'd also have sex with anyone
available. He'd get mad and hit me. Again, I said
nothing. I felt I deserved it. I'd usually pass out
before the night was over and someone would have
to take me home. Finally the band got sick of my
myriad of problems. They kicked me out of the
group and were right to do so—I was a walking
disaster.

Now, with nothing to hold me back, I decided
to run away to live with a friend in a commune in
San Diego. It was in a big, old, run down, three-story
home that sat on the edge of a canyon that was
crossed by a big suspension bridge. I'd get high and
go out in the middle of the night and swing on that
bridge. Weird. I also went to a self realization
fellowship; everyone in the commune belonged. It
was just another example of my search for
something deeper. And while I enjoyed myself there,
the members of the commune eventually asked me
to leave. Someone had found out I was a 17 year-old
runaway, and they didn't want to risk the cops
coming around (because of the drugs they kept).

I remember walking up the street to the 7
eleven and calling my mom from the pay phone. She
only asked where I was, then came and got me. My
eating and hygiene had been sporadic to say the
least, and suffice it to say I had various forms of
vermin. Upon returning home, mom got me all
cleaned up, took me to the doctor, got me treated and
even protected me from my family.

A religious friend of my mom's by the name
of Emma Lee (I call her my God Mother as kind of a

joke, because she's into God and she's been like a second mom to me.) sent a young man named Mark to see me. He was a musician, a reformed druggie, a born again Christian and also very good looking. So, of course, I immediately fell for him.

Life was less complex, so eating was much better. I also felt safe, but I still had the "Anorexic Voodoo" going on. Mark would take me to his Presbyterian Church and youth groups. I even got baptized in the ocean at 18, because I wanted to change and because I wanted to impress Mark. It was just my luck he was already seeing someone and that they eventually married. This broke my heart.

I still wanted to change, so I went back to school, got my GED, gave up smoking, drugs and alcohol and worked on stopping the bulimia. There were some bad experiences where I couldn't throw up the food I'd binged on—so terrifying, in fact, that it was easier to just starve. The coffee ritual actually began during this period, because I didn't have privacy anymore.

I graduated from junior college. Both mom and dad were proud of me. I kind of liked that feeling. So I decided to go to college.

Point Loma Nazarene College

The school chosen was the Point Loma Nazarene College. It was a Christian college. I majored in

81

psychology and minored in literature. I was a
member of the honour society and even met a young
man (Marvin) with whom I felt safe but who I
wasn't really interested in.

Marymount College

One summer I went to Marymount College in
Palos Verdes, just as a different experience. I was
still somewhat peculiar, but I was learning how to
make friends. I was also doing well in school. I
suffered terribly from bowel problems, though. Two
hours per day, between four am and six am, were
taken up with bathroom issues. This was to keep safe
and have privacy. I'd drink two cups of coffee and
two cups of water then try to go to the bathroom.
After this I'd go running. It gave me predictability. I
had to be in control, you see. I was very rigid,
exceedingly so. I envy people who don't keep
schedules.

A week before finals, on a Wednesday in my
last year, I was called by the women's dean to the
front of the chapel (we had chapel every day before
school). I wondered why she called me up there and
said I was needed at home immediately. I had a
feeling it was something to do with my dad. He'd

already had one heart attack in his 40s. Turned out I was right. Dad was dead at age 57 of a heart attack. Mom and the boys were sitting in the kitchen when I arrived. I didn't feel anything. I wasn't even there, was just watching.

This is what the disease does to you. It pulls you away, and you're always apart. I went back to school after the funeral, wrote finals and graduated cum laude. No one even knew my father was dead.

My first job was as a waitress at Nordstrom's, but I eventually landed an internship as a social worker at a local convalescent hospital. I had an inherent gift for working with the elderly, especially those who suffered from Dementia or Alzheimer's. This was only an internship, but I did so well I was asked to take a job that came up. I jumped at the chance. At this time I lived at home. Life was routine.

Eileen and Daroush

Then I met an Iranian named Daroush. He was studying to be a CPA, and he was gorgeous. I broached the subject with mom, but she was dead set against me seeing anyone from that part of the world. At the time Greg was a Naval aviator stationed in the Persian Gulf. However, I was unable to resist my boy friend's exotic looks and charm, and I saw him in spite of my mother's objections. For his part, he was unwilling to continue the relationship without my mother's approval. After various attempts to negotiate between my mother and I, it became obvious that nothing was going to change, so he left me. Broke my heart.

Not long after I decided to try living in an apartment away from home. I was introduced to a young woman named Kathy through a friend of Emma Lee's. She was looking for a roommate. It wasn't long, however, before my rituals and obvious dysfunction both alarmed and annoyed my new roommate—to the point that Kathy periodically called my mom asking what to do. It was finally decided that I should return home.

Greg during the Gulf War

Chapter 8

"The addictive personality..."

Early Clapton

I've noticed the more spiritual I become the more I see that while addiction acts as a security blanket or even a protective shield it also ends up being your torturer. It turns on you, attacking you, biting you and letting others do the same. There's a song from the 1960s called *Come Down Off Your Drum* by *Blind Faith*. One of the verses has always stayed with me "Come down off your throne and leave your body alone." It speaks to the kind of relationship I have with my body. I can never leave it alone, and I don't listen to it. It's like a

85

slave/master relationship. It often begs me to leave it alone, but I refuse to listen. I remember seeing a comedienne on the Comedy Channel. She said, "I went to see my psychiatrist this morning and we finally figured out what my problem is. The problem is I'm a piece of shit that the universe revolves around." That paradox is the best description for the way I view myself. I feel inferior and unacceptable in every way, and yet I expect others to understand, listen to and care for me. My mother filled that roll, as did my doctors and the few carefully selected friends I had.

What finally happened after many years of mom and I being cut off from society, where nobody could penetrate the wall we'd constructed—Jeff tried, but he couldn't get through to us—was that disaster struck. It was on a Good Friday about four or five years ago. We went out for Mass at this place called Prince of Peace Abbey, near camp Pendleton, and as we often did on special holidays we stopped at a shop called Coco's to get pie for Easter.

While there, Mom said she had to sit down. All the life seemed to drain out of her. But after a little while she said she was okay, so we went on to an appointment I had with my psychiatrist (mom almost always came with me to my medical appointments). Dr. Hintz noticed how mom looked and said to me that she thought my mother had experienced a mini-stroke and that she needed to go to the hospital. But mom refused to go. At this point I suggested why not make an appointment to see her own doctor on Monday. Mom agreed, and it turned out she had experienced a TIA (a Transient Ischemic Attack or mini-stroke, the symptoms of which tend to last for about 24 hours).

Now, mom had an existing blood condition— Polycythemia Vera, a slow-growing type of blood cancer in which your bone marrow makes too many red blood cells. It may also result in production of too many of the other types of blood cells (white blood cells and platelets). These excess cells thicken your blood and cause complications, such as a risk of blood clots or bleeding [and hence strokes].[9] The medication required for the condition had terrible side-effects, but mom was long-suffering and rarely complained.

The Blue Angels

As mentioned, when Monday arrived, Mom's doctor confirmed the TIA. Yet, where she should have fully recovered, in the weeks after the appointment I began to notice mom was slipping, was forgetting things. Then, when we were on a drive to the Miramar Naval station (which is the former TOPGUN training school and is also near the

[9]**Data taken from the Mayo Clinic website**

annual winter training site of The Blue Angels at NAF El Centro, California), we were broadsided by a transport truck as we were about to exit onto the ramp leading to the naval station. Luckily mom was able to retain control, and we continued onto the ramp and up to the guarded entrance to the camp. A guy on a motorcycle came over, explaining to us that he'd seen the whole thing. He was a navy seal who was so nice he ended up reporting things for us. I think the accident was a combination of mom's problems and the transport driver not paying attention.

We told the boys, who were already concerned about mom, what had happened. My brother Greg, a pilot for Delta Airlines, arranged for a flight to San Diego and stayed overnight with us. It became obvious to him that mom was slipping. He called Jeff and told him that mom was in a bad way. Jeff talked to Doctor Calabro, who told him the scaffolding of our relationship was coming undone and that an intervention was needed. Together they arranged for a day nurse to come in and help.

Mom and I viewed this as an intrusion. We resented the interference with our usual routines. The whole situation was very uncomfortable. Oftentimes we would hole up in mom's room while the nurse would watch television in the den.

The result of all of this was that very slowly I began to slip, dropping about a pound a week. This did not escape the notice of my psychiatrist. She began to weigh me weekly and finally gave me an ultimatum. She said unless one of two things happened she would no longer be my psychiatrist. One, I had to turn my weight loss around or, two, I must go to the hospital to get help. "Eileen," she said, "this is a very delicate web you're resting on. What if something happens to your mom? There's no way you can handle living on your own, and I fear for you. That day will come, Eileen—what will you do? I can't in good conscience be an enabler to you."

She kept her word. When I didn't make any changes in a month, she stopped seeing me. It was then I began to lose weight fast, getting down into the 50s. I'd also lost my mind. I was completely out of it, crying all the time. This would be in 2010. Things got so scary I finally called UCLA for help (Dr. Hintz had given me the number in that final month before I left her office), and a friend took me for a tour of the facilities.

Dedicated to providing caring and comprehensive treatment

for children, adolescents and adults with eating disorders

UCLA Eating Disorder Treatment Program

The woman giving the tour was named Maureen. I had spoken to her by telephone several times before finally making the decision to take the tour. My friend, Sherrye, who'd been a hired as a companion for me and who was also in communication with my brothers, drove me to Westwood to take that tour. At the conclusion of the tour, Maureen asked if I'd like to be put on the waiting list. I turned to her and said, "Truthfully, I'm worried if I go home I might change my mind, and I've been having chest pain." Maureen said, "Look, I can get you in today, but you have to go down to the

ER." Sherry made me feel okay with this by saying she would bring me my clothes and stuff from home. They were great at the ER. My doctor was so cool, I just loved him. Everyone was nice; I was overwhelmed by how good they were. It was March 2010.

When I got up on the unit, I was shocked to find out my weight had gotten down to 59 pounds. I was also freaking out because I'd missed my dinner. After being checked in by the nurse, Lisa, my nutritionist, came in and sat on my bed and explained what I could and couldn't have, then she went down to the kitchen to get it for me. It was 6:30 by the time I ate, and while I was crying, on some level I felt safe, safer than any time since my mom had become ill. In time, I actually began to feel like I never wanted to leave.

The staff was very good to me, but when I got to 76 pounds I freaked out, even though it was unreasonable, even though Dr. Strober came to me saying, "Eileen, nothing good ever comes from panic." The truth was every pound I gained represented loss—loss of control, loss of my mother and loss of UCLA as my safe haven. Even Chandler, my therapist, begged me not to leave. But I said, "Please, please don't hate me. I can't go any further."

I saw my world crumbling. I felt that if I didn't get out of there, it would be the end of me. So I rented a car (against doctor's orders and the wishes of everyone else) and drove myself home. Both my mom and the nurse who was taking care of her knew I was coming home, and they came out onto the patio to greet me. Mom put her arms around me saying, "I'm so glad you're home." She looked like this fragile little bird with a faraway look in her eyes. It was a look that told me I was losing my mother.

The nurse seemed nice enough and was glad to see my mom happy. But after I'd made dinner, the nurse left us, saying she would return the next day. I immediately stiffened, remembering the home I'd returned to was no longer the home mom and I had known through all these years. Deep in my being I felt a sliver of panic. Home was no longer a safe place to be.

The days went on in sort of a cat and mouse game between mom, me and the nurses. We would ensconce ourselves in one part of the house, while the nurses retreated to another part. We also explained to the nurses that we didn't want them to come into the kitchen while were in there, because we wanted our privacy.

It wasn't all bad, though, as the nurses took us on many outings—to the sea or for drives and even to our appointments. But there was always intrusion. And I wasn't stable, so much so that it became apparent after just a few months that I was slipping. So was mom.

I also scared myself, because I began to lose my patience with mom. She would often put things away, like my glasses, then forget she had ever done so. Jeff and I were on the phone almost daily; I was usually hysterical.

It wasn't long before I realized I should never have left UCLA. So, I decided to call Maureen and get readmitted. It was late June or early July, 2010 when I returned to UCLA for the second time.

The staff was still very good to me, but when I got up to 80 pounds, I once again began to freak out. I didn't know why, which is the nature of the beast. But the truth was the same. The truth was that every pound I gained represented loss—loss of the only world I'd ever felt safe or secure in.

I began to talk to Chandler, my therapist. I was in a complete panic and wanted to get out of UCLA. I began to exercise in my room. Dr. Strober said to me, "Eileen, don't worry. We won't let your weight go beyond ninety pounds." He tried to assure me that no one was trying to take anything away from me.

The goal was to get me to a low but medically stable weight. But finally, after two weeks of going backwards and forwards, he said, "It seems mutually agreed upon that there's no point in you staying."

I'd gone as far as I could go. So in early September of 2010, I left UCLA for the second time, having achieved a higher weight than in my previous stay but having fallen short of the intended goal.

Arriving at home, it was readily apparent that things were still deteriorating with mom—despite the daily visits from nurses. In a short time it had a great effect upon me. My birthday was October first. Mom had always made it a very special day. I'd expected the same this year. But as my birthday arrived, I discovered my mom had forgotten. Not only was I heartbroken, I ended up spending the day at the DMV renewing my driver's license. In retrospect it was unrealistic of me to expect anything from that poor little bird.

As my own health once again began to slide, my ability to cope with mom lessened. There were more hysterical calls to Jeff and more disagreements and meltdowns with the nurses.

Then there was the instance where I'd lost my temper and almost hit my mom. I called Chandler about it—she was still my therapist—and she, in turn, called APS (Adult Protective Services). They came to the house, and mom told them everything was fine, that it had been a misunderstanding. The incident really frightened me. I'd been shown both mom and I were in trouble.

Things went on like this for awhile. We made it through Thanksgiving and Christmas. Then, on New Year's Day, I began to feel weak and my blood pressure was high, so I spoke with an on call doctor. He told me to take some medicine, which didn't work. He then told me to go to the ER at Scripps Hospital, which I did. I told them I thought I was having a heart attack, and they immediately took me to the back. I called Jeff and he called Sherrye and she made arrangements for Mom to get home.

Scripps Mercy Hospital, San Diego

The doctors at Scripps decided it was dangerous for me to go home because of my low weight. They were also upset about the whole situation with mom and me. A social worker called Chandler and Jeff and they, in turn, talked Maureen into letting me return to UCLA two weeks from then when there was a bed opening up. Scripps agreed to

93

keep me until then. And because they treated me like royalty—I had a private room overlooking the Torrie Pines Golf Course where Tiger Woods once won a PGA tournament, and the food was gourmet—I didn't mind.

During my time at Scripps Jeff said, "We aren't going to do this anymore." Everyone involved decided that while mom and I were separated, Jeff and Greg would to move us to Atlanta. We had already looked at Huntcliff Estates, so they thought it was a perfect solution, especially since the assisted living home was only a mile away from Greg.

I was at UCLA from January until April, 2011. This time I went up to 85 pounds. Chandler was still seeing me, and I was doing pretty good. Except that I'd begun clandestine running in my room when I crossed the 80 pound mark.

UCLA thought the reason I kept relapsing was because of the situation with mom, so with everything in place, they moved me to a day plan. But the first day out I went jogging and it just continued from there. I began to steadily lose weight and within two weeks it was mutually agreed upon that I should leave the program.
Greg picked me up at the airport, driving mom and me to Huntcliff. However all the furniture was in a big pile in the living room, so we lived like that for a week until Jeff and Jackie flew out to help us. Just another opportunity Greg and Nancy had to nice, but they couldn't be bothered.

The dining room at Huntcliff was fantastic, like living at the Four Seasons Hotel. There was a hostess, and everyone dressed for dinner. We could order off a menu. And every night waiters brought around a dessert cart.

There were outings and many activities. We even joined The Red Hat Society for ladies, which is

The Huntcliff Dining Room

a big thing in the South. Mom and I'd usually watch
TV in the evening. It was just so easy—to resume
my usual routine of going to bed early, to wake up at
four am to perform my usual rituals and to go
running.

There was one big wrinkle. Mom was
sundowning (a condition in Alzheimer patients
where they're more confused and agitated in the
evening) and sometimes in the middle of night she
would get up, throw the suitcase on the bed and
would start packing to go home. I'd try to talk mom
out of these midnight journeys. But she would push
and yell and try to hit me. Sometimes, I'd push back.
Then I'd go out on the patio and smoke and cry. I
was soon at wits end. Everything familiar was gone:
my mom, my car, my cat, my doctors, my home and
my routine.

When I told Greg and Jeff what was going on,
they accused me of being a drama queen. My
relationship with Greg and his wife became
exceedingly strained.

I started to tank again, and the daily phone
calls to Jeff resumed. Even the woman in charge of
social services at Huntcliff mentioned to my brothers
her concern about my weight and emotional state
and about the health of my mother.

It was decided I should resume therapy. We were lucky to find a local therapist by the name of Tammy Holcomb. She was alarmed by my weight and encouraged me to check myself into Emory Hospital ER. But Greg and Jeff chided me, stating, "Here we go again with the hospitals. Wash, rinse, repeat; Wash, rinse, repeat."

I did eventually go into Emory, but I signed out within one day. They wouldn't let me drink coffee, which you know by now is part of one of my major rituals. Everyone was furious.

Tammy decided to try the team approach. She hooked me up with a nutritionist named Page Love. She's the go-to nutrition consultant in Atlanta for eating disorders, and she's the nutrition consultant for the U.S. Olympic tennis team and the Atlanta Braves. Page and Tammy talked, then told me about Kris, a recovering Bulimic, who had a company

SOAR
Supporting Others Achieve Recovery

called Soar and who acted as a recovery coach. Kris ended up functioning as a companion who was with me when I went to my doctor appointments, when I went shopping, when I ate (talking to me about my menu as we went along) and who tried to get me to stop running, all the while doing the same type of refeeding they did in the hospital. She also noticed the dynamic with mom and talked to Page, Tammy and Jeff, saying that mom needed a higher level of care and that I needed to be on my own to learn some independent living skills. She made a special point of mentioning I wasn't able to cope with mom's increasing dementia.

Kris then found an assisted living place for me (Dunwoody Pines), which was about fifteen minutes from mom. The hope was that without me there my brothers would finally see what was going on with mom.

And that's what happened. When I did move, it became increasingly evident mom wasn't okay. She was always asking where dad was, she couldn't dress properly (her clothes were often mismatched, she would put her bra over her top, she would come out with her blouse undone and she would talk about the baby she was taking care of). It was soon clear that mom required a higher level of care specifically designed for people with dementia. Huntcliff had a small, attractive house behind the apartment complex for such cases. It was called Sunrise. They even had a secure floor for the worst cases. Mom moved into Sunrise in the early spring.

I was at Dunwoody until the end of December, at which time we found an incredible apartment for seven hundred dollars per month. I was so excited. It overlooked the Chattahoochee river and was so beautiful. Kris was going to help me every day. The goal was to get me to live more independently.

But Kris quickly saw that I was losing weight. And she realized the whole thing about decreasing my dependence on her wasn't working, that conversely it was actually increasing my dependence on her. I was using her to replace mom. Finally, Kris called Jeff and said she wasn't coming back. She also stressed the fact that I needed help. She was really concerned. "I don't want to come in and find her dead," she told Jeff.

My brothers were so mad at this point that
they couldn't have cared whether I lived or died. No
one understood that I was lost for mom, and I kept
thinking if I got sick enough mom would come back
or someone would swoop in to take care of me. The
problem was I'd been so protected by mom that I
didn't understand the real world.

In desperation, Jeff called UCLA. And even
though Chandler was no longer a therapist there, he
did everything he could to get them to take me back
for the fourth time. So, in May of 2012 I entered
UCLA for my fourth and final visit. I was 58 pounds
and having cardiac problems. They put me on forced
bed rest (there was even a bed alarm). Then I was
assigned a nice therapist. Her name was Dr. Cindy
Pikus. She was the assistant director of the adult
eating disorder program.

I really tried to follow directions, but as they
increased the calories I was eating, I once again
began to panic. My mind was overwhelmed. It drove
me to wake up in the middle of night and obsess
about the food I'd eaten that day. The panic I was
feeling eventually led me to disarm the alarm, to get
out of bed and to exercise. This was about two
weeks into my stay.

I'd been on forced bed those first two weeks.
But now I was allowed back into the general
population. Dr. Strober was watching me closely,
though, and one day after group therapy he asked me
if I was alright. I said I was fine, but I was terrified
that he might know about the exercise. He walked
away. Then he turned around, came back and said,
"So, Eileen, if a tree falls in the forest and there's
nobody there, does it make a sound?" I didn't know
what he was getting at, so I just shrugged. He
walked over to the nursing station then came back
again, saying, "If Eileen is exercising in her room

and no one sees it, is she really exercising?" Then he walked away for good. I was flabbergasted.

It wasn't long after this I confessed to my therapist I was exercising. She said "That's what we suspected." So I promised her I'd stop, but by then the monster already had its tentacles around me, and I just … couldn't … do it. So, while I did make progress it happened slowly. My doctors wanted to get me to a stabilized weight of 80-85 pounds. They told me they would be happy with that. The idea terrified me.

Now, my insurance company had been paying for this all along, but they weren't going to continue to do so if I wasn't going to get better. And sure enough, in July of 2012, they said to my therapist, "This is the fourth go-around with this woman and you say she's exercising, that she's repeating the pattern, so we suggest you discharge her." They were willing to pay for a lower level of care, but my BMI (Body Mass Index), which is a measure of body fat based on height, was too low to qualify for a residential program/halfway house—no one would take me.

Jeff decided there would be no more of this. He was done. So he did the only thing he could think of and brought me to Rhode Island to live with him. I immediately began losing weight. His wife, Jackie, was furious. They got me into an outpatient program at Butler Hospital. But I was still running, so I continued to lose weight in their program. Then they tried putting me into an assisted living program at night, called Epic. I stayed there then walked next door to the outpatient program each the day. I, of course, got kicked out for non-compliance. The doctor recommended I be admitted to a hospital again.

In August, after speaking with Page, Jeff and I left Rhode Island and flew into Atlanta. We stayed at our usual spot, a Holiday Inn Express. While we were there, we went to a place called Ridgeview (Page had made arrangements for me to be admitted there) and went through all their screening. After sitting and waiting for hours, they came to us with the news I'd been turned down, saying I needed to be in a hospital, that I was physically unsustainable.

We spent the night at Greg's house. They desperately decided that going forward I'd stay there with Greg and Nancy. I said, "No way," even though I could see mom every day. I begged Jeff not to leave me. The next morning, Greg said nobody cared what I did. Run, don't eat, see mom, nobody cares. It was like they were saying go ahead and die.

It was awful. I hated cooking for myself, and while I was allowed to use the fridge, Nancy didn't want me in the kitchen. It was worse than awful. She asked me to not be around when the kids were getting ready for school, and they never ate dinner before eight pm, which just didn't work with my schedule. I began to have bathroom problems, and I ran in the dark because I was ashamed of doing that. I was seeing mom, but the nurses were telling Greg that I was making her worse. And it was true. My visits were leaving mom visibly agitated.

One day the home said no more. They wouldn't let me see mom. My stomach dropped to my knees. I was in total shock. The entire reason I was back in Atlanta was to be with mom. I had no more reason to live, as everything I loved was gone. The darkness was closing in.

When I went home and confronted him, Greg pretended like he didn't know I was going to be banned from seeing mom. Then that night I overheard Nancy say she wanted me gone, that the kids wanted me gone. Greg's answer was at the rate she's going she won't be around long anyway.

I ran away to a hotel room, the place Jeff and I always stayed. A voice in my head said you don't want to be here, Jeff and Greg don't want you, your doctors don't want you and you can't even see your mom. I went to a pharmacy and bought a bottle of sleeping pills, but I couldn't bring myself to take them, mostly due to my experience when I was fifteen. So, I took the pills back and talked with the pharmacist. She said if I had anyone at all I should call them. I got in touch with a friend of mine named Kim, and she said I could stay with her at JUST PEOPLE, a persons-with-disabilities community in Atlanta.

But I was just a wreck. Page was trying to get me into Acute Care in Colorado. My psychiatrist was also trying to find a hospital. Even the councillors at Just People were trying to help me, but I kept going downhill. Becky Dowling, the manager, finally called Jeff out of concern that I'd die on their property (she and Jeff had been in contact from the get go).

Jeff flew into Atlanta on his birthday and took me home with him. At this point I was physically done. My brain was shutting down and my body wasn't functioning. Within a week I'd alienated the whole family to the point where I even ruined Jackie's birthday. It was then they put me in an assisted living program at Epic, the only place that would take me. At the end of October, five days after being admitted, I collapsed. I went into Rhode Island hospital for a month, until they found out Johns Hopkins in Baltimore would take me.

And so we begin again.

Eileen Rand

PART TWO

Odds & Ends

(This part of the book reflects an evolutionary process from the beginning of this project when Eileen was emotionally distraught, angry and confused, to the latter sections where she appears to be making peace with God, herself and the people in her life—past and present)

Eileen Rand

Chapter 9

I'm so alone. I wish Jeff could understand that all I need is support—unconditional love and someone to hold me. I haven't been touched since I was with mom.

A Lonesome Tree

My approach to getting well: it's not something you can force. It happens in God's time, not my time. You can't force a kindergarten pupil into high school, and you can't force yourself to get well. There has to be a process, a learning process, and it's different for everybody. For some people it's hitting bottom, but for me it's like I'm in this season in my life—I'm being isolated from everything and everyone. I'm having a lot of time alone, to learn the things I need to learn, to reflect, to see the function of this illness, to see its purpose. Anorexia was a survival tool for me, and now I'm being instructed by the Holy Spirit on how not to need that tool.

Things go of their own accord. Nothing happens in nature without a reason. This is a time of stripping away; acid poured on glue. It's lonely but necessary. It's dark. You don't know if you're going to make it.

My rituals helped me. I had nothing else other than my mom, who passed away September 4th, 2013. Everyone including me thought I was going to implode.

I do, of course, miss California. There was a lot to do there. I could go to the beach. There were all these neat places I could shop. I could even go into Hollywood. Then there's the cemetery where mom's buried. It's a grassy knoll with plaques in the ground, and a pond and aspen trees with a wind chime. Chinese people will have parties right in the cemetery when it's someone's birthday. On a child's grave they leave stuffed animals and candies on their birthdays.

My own birthday is October 1st, 1964. And when I look at myself in the mirror, I wonder if it's possible that I'll ever look normal again. I wear every year of this disease on my face. Yet, in order to change I must go through this underneath the soil process of being a seed; I won't know what will happen when I make it through to the sunlight, if I make it through.

This is my process, and I have to have patience and tolerance. Like when I was in the hospital last year, I had the emotional security of a

106

seven year-old but I'm almost 50. I'm reminded of that quote from the Bible, "When I was a child I thought and reasoned like a child, but when I became a woman I put away childish things."

Eileen as a child

Eileen Today

ભ

I'm seeing a naturopath. Jeff and Jackie don't like me to see those they call witch doctors, but I don't like traditional medicine. I used to go weeks without going to the bathroom, and all they (the doctors) wanted me to do was eat. I'd tell them if I could crap, then I could eat. People don't understand that. I'd be force fed 3,000-4,000 calories a day, but I'd be going five to seven days without having a bowel movement. My rituals would help with this. If I could only do them, then I would be all right.

I remember going to this naturopath who said my eyes indicated I was full of waste. The brown around my irises told him the small and large intestines were in trouble. I took some stuff to help. I was able to go to the bathroom every day. But even now that my eyes are better there are still problems with my intestines. I'm better but not cured. I have this solid brown mucous that comes out. I have inflammation and yeast and fungal infections.

ભ

The food at Cortland is hearty food, but not healthy food. So, I get the makings for a salad every day. I like food. Most Anorexics love food. I think about food twenty-four/seven. I think about it, I plan for it, I obsess over it. I talk to my nutritionist, I study the menu and mark the things I'm going to eat.

ભ

God is teaching me to focus on my life, and he's teaching me about my life and how to run it. The more I focus on living my life the way he wants me to, the more everything falls into place. But, the more I try to plan, the less control I actually have and the more fear I have. I need to renounce my fears, because when I live right, I find I feel better.

I can't see what God has in store for me today—this used to baffle me, but now it makes more sense. I was being forced into my "Self." Now it's just me and God. I don't have my mom anymore. I'm all alone, so I call on him often.

ଓ

All the years of this illness, I wear it on my body, on my person, and I can't escape that. There's no hiding it. Every time I look in the mirror it shocks me, because what I remember is this little girl. And I don't know if I'll ever get that back. Yes, I'm learning to trust and that I can't force things. But that trust is all I've got. And it hurts.

ଓ

Jackie said, "You're part of our family."
I said, "But you don't understand me."
She replied, "We don't need to understand you to have you as part of our family."
Then I went to see my therapist on Tuesday. I was telling her how I couldn't make up my mind as to whether or not I should go over to Jeff and Jackie's home for Easter. I get overwhelmed by all of the food. And sure enough, now that it's done, I've been over-exercising and under-eating all week. It's because I'm so ashamed of how much I ate on Sunday.

My mother and I had a system. We would get up and have a little breakfast, go to mass, then come home and have a little salad and relish tray and a roll. Then we would go back out for a walk. And dinner would be very basic food groups. But at Jackie's house … it's antipasto, pasta, soup, and then the main meal. There were meatballs and sausage, ham, lamb, stuffed artichokes, risotto, roasted vegetables, potatoes, sweet potatoes and six types of pie for dessert. Even though I just took a little bit of everything, it will take me weeks to get over this, especially because I feel like I've done something wrong.

CR

I hate Rhode Island. I think most of the people who live here hate Rhode Island. It's the smallest state in the country, it's provincial and it's economically depressed. We have the highest unemployment rate in the union, and more people leave here than come every year. There are a lot of immigrants: Cape Verde, Africa, Portugal, and Puerto Rica. People have a pretty rough attitude. Whereas I've mentioned when I'm in California there are always people to see and something to do.

But to project is useless. In Exodus, Moses led the people into the desert. They quickly tired of the quail Moses provided for them, so God sent Manna from the heavens. But he said, "You can't horde it." The goal is that you trust God to feed you each day. Some of the people didn't listen, and as God promised the food became infested with maggots overnight and gave off this horrible smell.

I've stopped projecting. And I don't horde food anymore, because God is teaching me that I don't need it. God's lesson is Manna for the day!

CR

I got in a car accident this week because I wasn't in the moment. I was thinking about this and about that. I'd begun projecting again.

ɢ

When I was in my early 30s, I'd been in and out of quite a few hospitals. Then I was at this new hospital, and I remember I was screaming and freaking out. They, in turn, were pouring ensure down my throat. I ran outside in my nightgown and it opened up. But I got to the side of the freeway. This guy in a van got out and began to try to drag me into his vehicle. Then this really nice woman scared him off. I told her I was trying to get home to San Diego to my mom. The woman thought I was a child. She gave me money and put me on the bus and called my mom so that she would be there to pick me up.

Then there was the time I'd been put on a Nose-Gastric tube—and they would feed me at night whatever I didn't eat during the day. I would scream and cry and pull out the tube or turn off the machine. One time, I ran off into the desert in the middle of the night.

ɢ

These memories are all very sketchy in my mind. Jeff will tell me something and I don't remember it or, sometimes, I'll get a little hazy picture like a watercolor. Part of this is due to hydrocephalus that I suffered before I went into Johns Hopkins (this was a result of severe starvation). It may also be due to the many ECT's I've had over the years.

111

Eileen Rand

Chapter 10

I would love going under...

I had a wonderful psychiatrist. I loved her.
She really understood me and my mom, and she had
a good sense of humour. But we weren't making
progress, so she pulled all my meds until we finally
settled on Prozac. I continued to deteriorate and
became despondent (my weight was now under 60
pounds). You feel like you're drowning—a dog
paddling to the surface, only to go back under again.
I got pancreatitis. It put me in the hospital. I went
down to 55 pounds while in the hospital and was still
losing. A woman named Dr. Susan Schuchter was
my doctor. She felt the hospital had done all they
could for me, so she decided to let me go home on
hospice. Home to mom and my lovely cat.
     Dr. Schwartz, rather than giving up on me,
talked to a colleague, Dr. Botkiss, who then
suggested electroconvulsive therapy (ECT) for the
depression. I went into the psych ward at Mesa Vista
hospital—it was just like the *Island of Misfit Toys*; I
fit right in there. I was merciless about teasing Dr.
Botkiss about his name. And the people, Marylou
and Dave in the ECT room, were wonderful and
would joke with me, and I'd love going under.

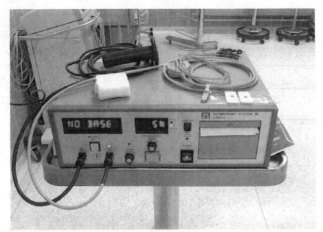

ECT Machine
www.boundless.com

When I woke up, I wouldn't remember anything. From there I went into observation. Within a week I was doing better. It was almost like I forgot I had an eating disorder. I gained ten pounds in two weeks.

This course of action initially took a load off mom, but they soon weaned me off hospice. It was decided that Sherrye at our church, All Hollows Parish, was to be hired to be my companion twice per week. She became a good friend.

ର

Electroconvulsive therapy (ECT) is a procedure in which electric currents are passed through the brain, intentionally triggering a brief seizure. ECT seems to cause changes in brain chemistry that can quickly reverse symptoms of certain mental illnesses. It often works when other treatments are unsuccessful.

Much of the stigma attached to ECT is based on early treatments in which high doses of electricity were administered without anesthesia, leading to memory loss, fractured bones and other serious side effects.

ECT is much safer today and is given to people while they're under general anesthesia.

Although ECT still causes some side effects, it now uses electrical currents given in a controlled setting to achieve the most benefit with the fewest possible risks.[10]

ଓଃ

Last night I dreamed I was at the courtyard at All Hallows, and I was strapped down on a bed in the dark, This man came down from the stairwell. I could see him in my mind's eye. He was all in black, and he was black. He had a knife, and I knew I was going to be tortured, and I knew I shouldn't have trusted.

ଓଃ

This illness is a way of screaming at people about the hurt I have inside and that I'm invisible. The illness helps me feel not so helpless.

ଓଃ

Seventh grade. This is where I really took this disease on and it took me on. The only price I had to pay to be treated right and to have people care about me was staying thin. But when your body is trying to

[10]http://www.mayoclinic.org/tests-procedures/electroconvulsive-therapy/basics/definition/prc-20014161

grow being hungry is awful. The one thing my whole day revolved around was dinner, and I knew there would be safety, order, perfection and that the food would be gourmet. We would all eat together. It's the structure and the safety my mother provided me over the years that kept me alive.

People just don't see it. They want to believe the two of us played off each other and created this terrible harmonic that kept us isolated. Let's suppose that's true, is the company I provided for her at a cost of outside influences such a great price to pay for my life?

I've been anorexic since I was 13 and now I'm 50. Everyone I knew who had this disease is cured or dead. There's no one like me. Mom knew that and didn't care.

Palomar Observatory
(www.astro.caltech.edu)

Anyway, it was about this time we began going to Palomar (Dove's Nest) again. It's where the observatory was. We had a cabin there, and I had a love affair with horses. I took lessons at the La Jolla Farms (they no longer exist). On my 13th birthday I was given a rescue horse. After getting Dusty, the horse from hell from Pecos (he was a mustang mutt), I taught him about people and he taught me about horses. Dad had a cousin who was dragged to death because he was hooked up in his saddle rigging, so he insisted I ride bareback. Greg had a sulky racer called King—very regal, seventeen hands. Dusty was about fifteen hands.

I was friends with Abigail Bergman, the daughter of one of the main landowners on Palomar Mountain. This gave me access to just about anywhere I wanted to ride. The Bergmans were cattle owners and the cattle were driven down to the Aguanga, Cahuilla Indian Reservation in the winter time and were brought back up in the summer. Dusty must have been part cutting pony, because instinct often took over when Abi and I would ride among the cattle and sometimes we even pretended we were on a real live cattle drive.

That's when I began to write about Annie (my fictional black stallion). It was another distraction from the hunger. Mr. Sylvester, who I previously mentioned, was known by all the kids as "Mr. Ed."

He was one of my teachers at that time. He took an interest in my writing and would read a chapter a week during seventh and eighth grade, at which time the starving and exercise was taking its toll. In fact, it took most of my time and all my emotional reserves. I knew the starving and the exercise was wrong but I couldn't stop. It was a secret, a secret, a secret.

Eileen on Palomar Mountain

[Transitioning to college now.] It was difficult to juggle my rituals. I lived on Campus, where there was no privacy. So, inevitably I was disturbed, and I couldn't get my bowels to release.

I previously told you that in 1987, on May 27th, one week past his 57th birthday, my dad died suddenly from a heart attack. He died on a Wednesday, and the funeral was on the Friday. I went back to school the next week and aced my exams. Dad's death really didn't affect me. I never cried for him.

CR

My jobs were always such that I was around food. But during my fourth quarter, I landed an internship at The Georgian Court Assisted Living Facility in San Diego. I worked in the locked Alzheimer's and psych ward. One of the younger guys, named Bob, was a war vet who had chronic alcoholism. We knew how to talk to each other. My job was to listen and report on the patients. I was good at what I did.

But I was always moody and when I moved in with Kathy Fiacco, a friend who is married now, she just couldn't relate to all my rituals. She called my mom and said Eileen is really having problems, and I can't deal with this. They decided I needed to come home. Soon my illness went on to interfere with my job and I quit. It wasn't long before Dr. Schwartz and Dr. Schucter asked me if I wanted to try the Remuda Ranch in Wickenburg Arizona. They said it wasn't a hospital environment but a warm, Christian, camp-like atmosphere—with horses. It also offered treatment for the severely anorexic (the part of the camp called Vista).

Eileen Rand

Chapter 11

She was my best friend, and she died.

Remuda was a Christian camp with a beautiful countryside. Really quite luxurious. It was there I met Cara. She was my roommate, and we both had an NG (Nasal/Gastric) tube.

I was nervous, but I was excited about the horses and the desert, and it made me think about all those books I'd read about *The Black Stallion*, the Bedouins, *The Arabian Nights*, the mystery, the gorgeous men and the Arabian horses, so delicate and so strong. Really, I've had a love affair with horses and the desert ever since I was a little girl.

I was also reminded of the time when we flew over to Flagstaff to go to the Grand Canyon. The Grand Canyon is one of the most beautiful and majestic things I've ever seen in my life. And that ride down the mountain on those donkeys? It was enough to raise the hair on the back of your head!

Anyway, Mom didn't fly to Remuda Ranch with me. They sent this special person to meet me and bring me back to the ranch. It's near this teeny, tiny town called Wickenburg. And it's way out in the middle of the desert. One of my councillors had a term for it that I can't repeat, so I'll just say it was the most remote place I've been, which I loved.

121

I was at a special location of the camp called Vista, which doesn't exist anymore. It was for the more severe cases. The reason it was separate was the remote cases needed a little more medical care. They went at a different pace than the other ranch. I went there a second time, so I've been to both camps.

I have memories of being on the plane. It didn't take very long to get there—only about an hour. I was picked up, and I settled in. The rooms were like a regular bedroom. There was a screen door that went out onto a little patio which looked out over the desert. There were a couple of buildings in this compound. I think we had a swimming pool, and in front of the Ranch House—it didn't look like a ranch house; it looked something like the Ponderosa from *Bonanza*—there was a lawn and then a lower level, with a building where the horses and the arena was. You had to earn the right to get on the horses.

The first week was spent just getting into the program. I don't remember a lot. The food was delicious, but there wasn't too much. When you go to a place like that they start you out very slow, because restoring weight is medically dangerous. I was only required to gain one to two pounds a week (That's safe. To try and do it any faster is dangerous). At Johns Hopkins the weight gain expected was three to five pounds per week, but I was told by one of the nurses that it was not uncommon for some of the girls to gain up to ten pounds in a week, which was horrific.

Remuda didn't offer acute care. There were doctors and nurses on staff, but this wasn't a hospital. If I was in the kind of shape I was in when I went to John Hopkins, they never would have accepted me. Anyway, there was a menu for each day. And the food was awesome. Being a Christian organization, they didn't give you more food than what you could handle. You were expected to eat what was given to you, but you weren't forced. If you didn't finish your meal, you were given Ensure as a replacement for what you didn't eat. In addition, if extra calories were required for proper weight gain, you got the NG tube at night. I always ate my food because I have a real thing about ensure: I hate it. I also got the NG tube for the prescribed weight gain.

I was scared. I felt like I was being whooshed through each day. Not knowing what was going on, I was just trying to cope. I was also uncomfortable; the body feelings that come up when you are refeeding are … the major issue for most of us is constipation. It's very difficult to deal with that when you're asked to eat larger quantities of food than your body is used to. Several things were tried for this—Metamusal and bran can make an anorexic worse, so they tried giving me Psyllium as an alternative. It made me worse. They ended up putting me on MiraLAX but that was a struggle the whole time I was there. I never did get regulated.

From the beginning I was given the NG tube. Well, it's one thing to eat the food, but it's quite another to have it drip into you. To me that's a total loss of control—a feeling of complete helplessness, which I fought.

"Why can't I eat these special ice cream thingies," I asked. (They were special, high calorie, ice cream cups. They call it a resource ice cream that has like 300 calories in it.)

They said no. But it was done in a nice way. They weren't ever harsh. I think it made a big difference that everyone was a Christian. To me it makes so much difference when people have faith. It changes people. We'd pray together and talk together. Our mornings would start with singing and praying before meals.

I was in my 30s and was older than most others. Even though Cara was just twenty-two, she and I became dear friends. We loved horses and both liked to run. She had this crazy thing about *The Flinstones*—anything to do with *The Flinstones* and me anything to do with cats and horses.

When you reach a certain point in Anorexia, your brain goes through changes. You begin to take on certain actions or rituals. This is why my previous doctor gave me the idea of Anorexic Voodoo. You make connections. For example, my day can't begin before I have my coffee, go to the bathroom and go running. Stuff like that. They're called rituals, and I had a ton of them. We all had crazy, little rituals. One of my peculiarities when I reach a certain weight is salt. I get really weird about salt. You see, your body's craving minerals. Naturally occurring

salt has lots and lots of trace minerals. I used to put salt on everything, even instead of butter. So, when I would go to eat they would only allow me a certain amount of condiments.

Common to anorexics are the overuse of condiments—like mustard, salt, artificial sweeteners of any kind, ketchup, soya sauce and at UCLA it was cinnamon—any condiment. You see, when you starve yourself you lose your sense of taste (this is due to the zinc deficiency we discussed earlier) so the condiments not only satisfy the craving for flavour but also give a sense of satisfaction to a stomach that is never full. It's also a belief that condiments won't make you gain weight. Then there's the fact that anorexics obsess about food. In fact, anorexics are paradoxical, the more power and control they gain (over their food, for example), the more out of control they can get.

Cara and I with our N/G Tubes

I was never overwhelmed at the ranch with regards to food. But I was constantly having meltdowns over my bowels, the NG tube and feeling fat and uncomfortable. The doctors even threatened to send me to a psych hospital. This created the emotional fear of being set up to be hurt again. I did, though, eventually earn the right to ride the horses.

Being at the ranch and meeting Cara (we were soul mates) meant a lot to me. She was repressed and her life force was drained, while I had a certain wildness and had some energy reserve. We were different but it didn't matter. We understood each other, that kind of unspoken understanding.

What happened to Cara (loss of life force) happens to many of us when we begin to eat again. Your body needs a lot of energy to digest food, and as anorexics tend to have very little energy in reserve, it puts you into what we called a food coma. You are so drained you just want to sleep.

Eventually, though, both Cara and I were assigned our own counselor for riding. She was like a farm girl and dressed the part, but she was also smart. She understood me pretty well, being a peer rather than one of the doctors.

I was given a horse named Barney. This drove Cara wild because of *The Flinstones* thing. But they wouldn't let us trade horses.

I loved this special time. It was all about getting out into nature, being free, feeling and grooming the animal, and just being a girl.

One day a Christian musician named Justin Knight came out to play for us. He gave us all a tape to listen to. I enjoyed this, as well.

Midway through, which was a month. They had parents week. And this is how Mary and my mother met. They really hit it off. Mary was gregarious and a devoted Christian. My mom was more quiet. Both had been counseled by family members to write off their daughters with eating disorders, and they had an understanding of each other and found support in each other. They also felt supported by Remuda. Even after my mother died, I kept up the relationship with Mary.

When mom came, she stayed for a few days and got some therapy. We also went to Scottsdale for shopping, which is what we do when I gain weight. I needed new clothes, and I love shopping. One of the reasons mom often indulged me was an underlying fear that I was on borrowed time. She was also hopeful that Remuda was turning things around for me. We both hoped it was the beginning of a new life for us.

But as good as the place was I wanted to go home. I bugged my mom constantly by phone until she gave in and brought me back. I went there at the beginning of September, 2003 and left at the end of the same October.

It was about one to two months later that Cara was found dead, in her apartment. Cara had gone to visit her father (he and Mary were divorced). The last evening she was there they went on a ten mile bicycle ride. The next day, a neighbour heard her vacuuming around midnight, so they know she was alive up to that point (Cara would often vacuum to help keep the voices out of her head). In the morning when her mother called there was no answer. She finally went over and found Cara, dead on the floor of her kitchen, food in the microwave and a book at one hand. Mary felt that since Cara's father was a doctor, he should have known better than to take an anorexic who had so recently put on weight on such a long ride.[11] Mary was heartbroken, but she was

[11]**From an interview with Mary Cavelli Johnson**

127

carried forward by her own faith. She said to my mother, "I have no regrets. I have no regrets. My little girl was sick and she needed me and everyone told me to walk away from her. If I'd walked away and this had happened, I would never have forgiven myself. And now that she's dead and with the Lord I can be at peace, because I did everything I could to save her. None of my time, the love and the patience I gave her was wasted, because she lived a beautiful life, and we had that special relationship and all those special moments. Also, she didn't die because she was a bad girl, she died because she had a nasty disease and it killed her."

These days Mary tells me that, every now and then, she gets little Flinstones messages that she believes are to let her know Cara is happy in heaven and that she's well.

Mary and my own mother's love and dedication has been criticized, and they have been judged harshly for enabling, which has some truth to it—I'll admit that— but there's no greater truth than pure, unadulterated love. Their love for their daughters was unconditional. They believed no human life should ever be wasted and that there's always another chance to forgive—one, two or 70 times. Just as in The Bible, where the Lord said, "No, seventy times seven." There is always another chance.

Speaking of the Bible and being judged, I need to get over whatever I'm hanging onto. That's what Jeff said to me yesterday.

I said, "Okay, I'll do it."

He replied, "No, don't say it, just do it!"

I said, "Okay."

So my goal for this week is to do it safely and gain a pound. I'll get off our administrator's case, quit fighting her and gain some weight.

Chapter 12

I'm not sure where the rest of this fits in, but it's on my mind, so I shall write it down.

My father lived like he was going to die young. He bought the finest of everything and things were done with great care and it was all provided for by hard work. I think Mom had the idea that when my father was gone the boys were going to pick up the slack. Instead, everything fell on her. Greg was only interested in his life, Jeff was away in College, and I was no help to anyone, not even myself.

Again I didn't react as one might expect. Death doesn't faze me. It's just a transition. Except that I'm afraid God is going to be mad at me when I go.

Mom eventually moved into a condo on Mount La Jolla. This was the time we became deeply involved in each other's life. Of course, at the center of it all was the disease. My illness fell on her shoulders, and she chose to take care of me.

ೞ

My brother Greg is someone I can't trust. This is someone I have to be very careful of, but I can't judge him. The lord must judge him. And God said

"I came back for the weak and the broken, for they can still be fixed, they can still be made whole." Here on the *Island of Misfit Toys*, that's what I believe: God can fix us, can make us whole. And even when I was homeless and living on the street that understanding was one of the most valuable experiences of my life. I'd been coddled and cared for by my mother or by hospitals or by doctors. Suddenly it was just me, in a sea of black people in an asphalt jungle. It was a kind of life I'd never experienced before. But God was with me; he fixed me to the point where I could deal with what lay ahead of me.

The Island of Misfit Toys

❦

Dr. Schwartz at UCSD had been seeing me for about fifteen years when she left her practice. We had been friends or at least comrades. We were both the same age, and we really got along. She sent me to Dr. Sonya Hintz, who was in private practice. She was much colder and distant than Dr. Schwartz.

Here I was looking for a new lifeline and Dr. Hintz was set on being distant. I tried giving her hugs at the ends of several sessions and Dr. Hintz finally said not to hug her.

Dr. Schwartz saw her patients as human beings. Don't get me wrong, Dr. Hintz was good. She was just more clinical. She even understood that mom and I were enmeshed and accepted it as a necessary evil. She never told me how she felt about it. I just went every week and spilled my guts. She encouraged me to change but I wouldn't take the bait.

During this time I also saw Dr. Susan Schuchter every two weeks. She was my medical doctor the whole time I was in San Diego. But it was Dr. Schwartz who saw both mom and me. It was good for mom to have someone to see her as well. She was under a lot of stress. I didn't realize everyone looked at me like a ticking time bomb that was certain to go off at some point.

℘

ECT with Dr. Botkiss. I saw him for two years, every two weeks for awhile, then we went down to a maintenance level of once per month. It was very helpful. My weight was stable at 69 pounds, and I was taking Prozac.

We took a trip to Greg and Nancy's place. They had an agenda and began to talk about us possibly living out there. During the first few days of our stay, Jeff and Greg took us on a tour of Huntcliff, a lovely assisted living facility less than a mile from Greg's home. Mom reluctantly agreed to the tour but was totally unimpressed and made sure that Jeff and Greg knew that there was no way we were going to leave our home in San Diego. Even so, Greg and Jeff insisted that mom and I continue to consider living in Atlanta. In the interest of remaining open minded, Mom said we must make sure that proper treatment for me would be available after such a move. So, Nancy found and took mom and me to a treatment center in Atlanta called Ridgeview. We took a drive out there the day before we were scheduled to return home to San Diego.

From **Ridgeview,** life starts to look manageable.

Ridgeview Institute is a private, not-for-profit provider of psychiatric and addiction treatment.

Now, outside of California I'm something of an anomaly, it being a kind of a haven for anorexics, so in Atlanta I got all these stares. The people at the home spoke to me, then they pulled mom and Nancy into another room and said, "Your daughter is very ill, and she should be in the hospital." We had just come to look at the place but they talked mom and Nancy into letting them keep me. I, of course fought it, but they kept me there at Ridgeview for two weeks.

Weird things happen when you have Anorexia. Like you can eat huge meals and not gain weight. Because your body goes into what they call hyper-metabolism. You're getting the food, but the internal organs are just sucking it down to start to rev up. The process/mechanism is trying to keep you alive before putting any flesh on your body. The staff at Ridgeview were feeding me well, but they wouldn't trust me to be alone, so I slept on a mattress on the floor in the hallway near the nursing station. It wasn't bad but it wasn't great. The girls there were sweet.

132

They used the food exchange program, so you don't count calories. I had freedom with the food exchanges—you know two bread, four protein and one fruit—and you could eat whatever you wanted within that framework as long as you met their weight gain requirements. After two weeks of gaining no weight, they said there was nothing else they could do.

I spent a horrible week with Greg and Nancy, then I went back to San Diego. While I was at Ridgeview the doctor had told me that for someone of my weight ECT could kill me. When I mentioned it to my doctor, he just shrugged and told me I'd signed papers that said I understood the risk. I stopped ECT, and I stopped taking Prozac. It was Easter time.

Once again, condemnation fueled my self-hate. These days I'm trying to like myself and look at myself as lovable. Everything I do is to fight the monster. I must learn that whatever I do, nothing is going to make God go away. All he wants me to learn is to love the way he does. I don't have to be perfect. I can go running and exercise and make many mistakes. It doesn't matter. God will still be there.

Eileen Rand

Chapter 13

She's having a heart attack!

The second time at UCLA I remember going with my friend Sherrye (the companion) at the end of February or in early March of 2010. I'll never forget it. They weighed me one morning, and I came in at 76 pounds. That was it. I told Chandler I wanted to go home. So, against everyone's admonitions I signed myself out, took a taxi to a car rental place, rented a car and drove home that night to San Diego. I had this illusion things would be the way they'd always been, but I was met by this nurse and my mother, and it just wasn't the old shoe I wanted to  put on.

Dr Chandler Sims Chang

A week later both Jeff and Greg approached a lawyer and began the process of taking over my mother's affairs. The big question was what are we going to do about Eileen? I, of course, still wanted to be taken care of. So it was agreed a nursing company called Lifeline would try to help me as well as mom.

Mother and I'd always had this delicate balance. She helped me without interfering with my disease. But the dynamic had changed this time round, which lead to anger and resentment, the very things that fuel this illness.

It got to the point where the nurses didn't want to help me because of my reputation, and they were telling me I needed to be in the hospital. I, in turn, insisted I was fine.

But my weight began to fall. I looked for help, and all I had was Jeff and maybe Dr. Schucter (She was just a nice, middle aged MD. A mom kind of a person, someone I could talk to.).

I was becoming more alienated and defensive, I was having outbursts, and I was getting angry with mom. She was constantly misplacing things, she couldn't drive me around, and I was trying to take care of her, doing the laundry and the cooking. But it was my temper that did me in. This is when the nurses called Jeff, saying I was becoming a liability to my mother.

By December my resources were drained. I was used to being pampered and cared for and cooked for and mom just couldn't do that anymore. But nothing was getting done. I had no therapist. We wouldn't let the nurses Jeff had hired come near us. We would retreat into the back of the house whenever they showed up.

When Christmas came around, I was down to 58 pounds. It was the last Christmas mom and I'd have together.

What happened to precipitate the next UCLA visit was I began to have trouble with my kidneys. I also developed high blood pressure. The day after New Year I became very ill. My blood pressure was 190/110 and it wouldn't go down, even with meds. I became very scared and began to have chest pains. When I called for help, I was told I to go to the emergency at La Jolla.

So, I put mom in the car and tried to call Jeff. The thing is he was just fed up with me. I had been calling him six or seven times a day, then acting out.

Anyway, at the hospital, they took one look at me, as emaciated as I was, and it was like, "Get this girl in here right now. She's having a heart attack!"

So mom's in her own little world in the waiting room, they take me into emergency and I think, "Who's going to look after her?" Well, I finally got through to Jeff, he called Sherrye and she came to get mom. This was at Scripps Memorial. They put me in the cardiac unit. They also got hold of my doctors, several who were associated with UCSD (University of California at San Diego).

I was there under observation. They wouldn't let me go home and were saying I really needed to be in an eating disorder program. After talking with my doctors everyone knew that if I went home I would be done. So a social worker got in on things, and she called Jeff and UCLA and they agreed to take me back one more time.

I was at Scripps Memorial for two weeks, then in the middle of January I went to UCLA. Sherrye drove mom and me. They call us frequent flyers up there. And every time I'd go, one of the girls from before was there. This time was no different. I also had Chandler as my therapist and Lisa Davis was my dietician. Also, to be truthful, UCLA felt a lot safer than being with mom. It felt like old home week. It felt like that old shoe.

Now, while I was in the hospital Jeff and Greg went, "Game over!" And by this time UCLA knew the whole dynamic between mom and me. They understood the gravity of the situation for both of us, that the relationship was dying and an intervention was of the utmost importance. I guess Chandler talked to Jeff about the fact that they had to get our mother out of the Condo. They would also have to get me to a place where I was no longer expecting anything from her. So, it was agreed that while I was in the hospital getting well—and this time they had my agreement that they would keep me until I'd reached my goal weight of a reasonable 80 pounds—they would find a place for mom to live.

All this was going on because Dr Strober thinks about people as individuals and works with them. He wanted to help the whole family. It was a very holistic program.

So what went wrong? UCLA probably has the best eating disorder program in the US. It wasn't anything they did. What went wrong was me. My disease. And a lot of naivety on my brothers' parts. I was there four months and made 85 pounds. That was four months they had to get mom out of the Condo and into Huntcliff, a nice sprawling place that is only a mile from where Greg and Nancy live.

Anyway, they did it. While I was in UCLA they moved my dear mommy out. By this time mom was like an innocent little girl. So sweet and good. Everyone who met her just fell in love with her. Except that mom wouldn't move into Huntcliff until I got out. She had to stay at Greg's place.

I know they wondered why, on 3,000 calories per day, it took so long for me to gain weight. Well, it was because I was secretly running, and I was exercising in my room. Lisa also said she had to put me on a higher calorie diet because, for some reason, each consecutive time you lose weight with this disease, you must eat more to gain.

There was this little girl there. She was just eighteen. They had to eventually put her on a four thousand calorie a day diet, because she was losing weight on a three thousand calorie diet. I was like that. And, of course, I loved it, because I got to eat all that gorgeous food.

Anyway, it was in April that it was decided I was going into the step-down outpatient program in May, which only lasts two weeks. I was excited, but I still felt lost and tortured. And this time when they dismissed me, Jeff was so exasperated. Here they'd done all of this for me, and as soon as I was released I was back to my old tricks—and losing weight again. Greg and Jeff were so tired of the wash, rinse, repeat business of my illness. It was wash, rinse, repeat; wash, rinse, repeat.

So I went home to the condo, and I got some dental work done. Two weeks later I flew into Atlanta. Greg left us at Huntcliff, but it wasn't until Jeff and Jackie came that mom and I were able to get settled in—they were wonderful. We had a one bedroom apartment that was very nice (we slept in the same bed). There was one bathroom, a kitchen, a living room, a den and a patio, but it was expensive and it was hard on both of us as mom was going into sundown syndrome. She would wake us up and want to pack to go home. When I tried to calm her down and get her to go back to bed, she would get agitated. Sometimes, she would hit me, and I'd cry and go out on the patio and smoke and wonder what on earth had happened to my life, to my mom, to everything.

We settled in as best we could. We did enjoy going to the beautiful dining room in the evening. Everyone would dress for dinner. It was the place to see and be seen. And there was a happy hour before dinner.

I wouldn't eat all day because the meals were so wonderful. It was like dining in a fine dining restaurant. It was the highlight of our day. We would put on jewelry and mom would wear her finest. Which was great, because she loved clothes and going shopping. The only problem was it took me an hour to get her dressed, as she needed help but was very particular. Once per week they had special outings. We went to see Margaret Mitchell's house. We went out with the Red Hat society to a famous restaurant called Aunt Pitty Pat. Atlanta is a beautiful place, and it has all these historic sites, and flowers and birds, and everything was lush and green. Except there were blue hydrangeas everywhere. Even the smell of the place was wonderful. You could also have your own garden patch. Mom and I sat on the swing and watched them work.

So our days—some of them were pleasant. I found a good therapist Tammy and my lovely, wonderful dietician Page, whom I still work with over the telephone. Page Love is her name (nutralove@gmail.com). She was the dietician for the US Olympic team and the Atlanta Braves.

ᘓ

Something to illustrate the relationship my brother Greg and I have. We rarely saw them. They would have mom over on Friday evenings and the weekends. I just couldn't go. They made me feel uncomfortable and, similarly, I made them feel uncomfortable. As I've mentioned they didn't eat until eight or nine at night, which just doesn't work for me.

Greg and Nancy flew to San Diego to tie things up with the condo, then they were going to drive both cars back to Atlanta so that mom and I could have our cars. I'll never forget this. We had gone out with the Red Hat's and then to a movie. My cell phone rings. I step out of the movie to answer it. Greg was calling me to tell me that they took my cat to the humane society.

"Nancy and I didn't want to have the cat crawling all over the car while we were driving home."

I said, "What!"

Then Nancy took the phone away from Greg and said, "Yeah! That's your fault."

I said, "What?"

She said, "Yeah. You were irresponsible. You left that poor cat in the house all by itself. That's not our responsibility. You should have thought of that before you left San Diego. That was your responsibility. We're not going to pick up the slack like your mommy did."

I went back into the theatre and was in tears cause they gave my dear, little Muffy away and blamed it on me. Of course I couldn't talk to mom about it. When I told her, she just went, "Oh, Muffy." I cried all afternoon. And when I told Jeff what Nancy said, he sided with them. He said that they weren't going to take care of me like mom did. Those days were over. That it was time to grow up, to start using some of the skills I learned at UCLA.

There was no communication at all. I could feel Jeff wincing on the phone every time I called,

and Greg has never responded to my calls or emails.
Jeff understands things, but Greg can't deal. It's
another case of not expecting people to know where
you are.

Chapter 14

"I know! If I just get sick enough, someone will rescue me."

I was incapable of comprehending that everything was gone. My mom, my home, my cat, UCLA. I was just staring into this big black hole. I somehow kept thinking, "I know! If I just get sick enough, someone will rescue me." This was not a conscious thought, but it was what was driving my behavior. So, once again I was on the road to destruction. I made a semi-conscious decision to get sick again. I was like a feral cat. And nothing was familiar. This was totally uncharted territory. No support came from Greg and Nancy. In fact, Nancy got strange. She began to be solicitous to mom, but I felt consciously excluded and increasingly unwelcome in their home.

At Huntcliff I was alarming the people in charge of our section. Mom and I were having yelling arguments. I was getting hysterical, and I was always crying. Not only that: I was losing so much weight people thought I had cancer. They were even starting to call Jeff. And Jeff was going, "Oh my God, oh my God. Here we go again."

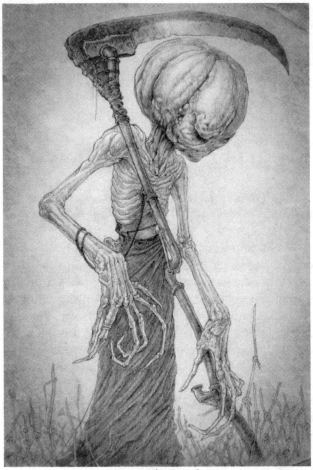

Anorexic Death

Mom and I'd been at Huntcliff since early June and it was now September. Barbara, the administrator was keeping tabs on us. She was the one who helped me to find Tammy Holcomb, a therapist in a town near us called Marietta. Tammy introduced me to Page the dietician, and they kept trying to get me back into some sort of program. The problem was no one would take me; I was too sick or too old or not sick enough.

They finally decided the best thing would be to take me to the ER at Emory Hospital. Greg picked me up and left me there. I was there for twenty-four hours before I was taken up to the Psych ward. After meeting with the psychiatrist, I found out I couldn't have coffee. I explained to him that I had to have coffee to go to the bathroom, but he said there would be no exceptions. He wasn't listening to me, and I wasn't listening to him, so I checked out. This, of course, not only infuriated Jeff and Greg, but the doctors and the people at Huntcliff who had facilitated my transfer to Emory. Jeff said it was almost like they were throwing me a lifeline, and I was refusing to take it. I'd succeeded in alienating anyone who might have supported me. It was a deteriorating, no win situation.

And that's when Page said, "Why don't we get this girl I know who's name is Kris who has recovered from an eating disorder and has started a company called Source. Kris would be my "recovery coach" and mom would have her own nurse. But after a couple of weeks, Kris made the observation that my being with mom was not helping either of us. Mom needed a higher level of care, and I needed to be in an assisted living situation on my own so that I wouldn't be responsible in any way for my mom's care. She figured it would then become clear to everyone what was really going on with mom. What could possibly go wrong?

Well, mom was getting worse and worse and worse, and I'm calling Jeff again and again and again, telling him what's happening and begging him to get me out of there. The long and the short of it is that in November I moved out to Dunwoody, the assisted living program.

145

But my problems continued to plague me, and it wasn't long before Kris and I were looking for apartments. We found one at Chattahoochee Landing. For seven hundred dollars per month (much less than assisted living) I got a porch overlooking the river and a great apartment. Kris would be spending a couple of days per week with me. What could possibly go wrong?

Well, for one thing, mom was completely lost without me. It was heartbreaking, because she was all alone in that apartment wondering where's my husband, where's my daughter. Wearing her bra overtop of her clothes, because she couldn't dress herself, and because no one had the time to deal with her. In the end she had to go to the dementia unit.

It was an annex, and was called Sunrise. They moved mom in there. But the boys were tired of moving me around. They were going, "Jesus, when is this going to stop?" They were getting burnt out.

I was working with Kris and Page and Tammy but, again, the only truly stable thing in my life was my eating disorder. In my mind, the only way for me to get the attention I wanted was to stay sick. Conversely, there was no motivation for me to get well. Kris would set goals and Page would set goals, but I kept losing weight. By May of that year, Kris said to Jeff "I'm not coming back, because I'm enabling her, and I'm afraid that one day I'll find her dead. I can't live with that."

I was now truly on my own. Everything I'd hoped would work had backfired. And yet that belief persisted: I'm just not sick enough.

Jeff then began to try to deal with the situation. We didn't even try to call Greg and Nancy, because I never saw them. Even though they only lived about a mile away, I never saw them.

I began to spend time with mom in the afternoons. I knew I was dying but I didn't care. Page was getting scared. She said she wanted to send me to this place in Colorado; it was called Acute Care. They wouldn't take my insurance, though, and we couldn't afford it. Jeff called UCLA and they said no. He then begged them (Dr. Strober) to reconsider, because if something wasn't done I was going to die. Page also talked to the new program director at UCLA. She was a beautiful young lady, a psychologist, dedicated, good of heart—just a kind, sweet woman. They said if the insurance will pay then Dr. Strober said we'll take you one last time.

Greg (it was May) picked me up the next day at four in the morning to take me to the airport. I weighed 57 pounds and had a huge suitcase. Do you know, he didn't even lift a finger to help me carry my suitcase? Greg made me drag my suitcase out of the apartment to the car. Then he popped the trunk open and waited for me to put the suitcase in.

I said, "I can't lift it."

He says, "God Damn it!" Then he gets out of the car and slams the door. Exasperated, he throws the bag in the trunk. He takes me to the airport, but because of the bag, I can't keep up with him. So rather than carry the bag himself, he gets a wheelchair for me and my bag. He drops me off, says take care of her, make sure she gets to LA and then he leaves.

On the plane I was sitting next to one of the Lakers. I told him where I was coming from and where I was going. He sat with me, got me a wheelchair, took me to a cab and said get her to UCLA emergency. He was a sweetheart.

I was quickly admitted, and this time they put me on strict bed rest with a bed alarm (so I couldn't exercise). There was to be no contact with other patients until they said I was ready to meet them. My bathroom door was locked. I had to buzz the nurses every time I had to pee. And I pee a lot when I'm gaining weight.

The staff was kind, good natured and treated me like a baby bird. This one black nurse from Jamaica, Miss Rose, would come in and say, "We take away your old clothes, we get you into the shower, then we put on your make-up and make you beautiful for the day," and "We take your vitals and we give you breakfast in bed," and "Oh ..."

Maureen (the director of nurses) wouldn't let me do anything. I wasn't allowed to participate in any groups. I saw the psychiatrist once a day. I saw the dietician once a day. I couldn't pick my own food at this time, but Lisa knew what I liked, so that was cool. Dr. Strober came in to talk to me. I had more attention than I could ever get at home. Even the young girls wanted to know the old timer. They would bring me little gifts and say "Hi Eileen, how are you?" And sometimes they would crowd around my door and ask questions and wish me well. I was a special kind of kitten.

I had no idea how bad I looked, but when one of the therapists came in to visit, she said to me, "I didn't know anyone could look like you and still be alive." And she said, "I'm just saying that Eileen, because I've seen you before when you were 85 pounds. What happened?"

My eating disorder speaks for me. My eating disorder knows more than I do. When secure and safe I can eat, when I don't feel safe I don't eat. It's how I get what I want. It's what keeps this beast in place.

Now I see myself going through the same process but consciously. This book is a process. I'm fighting the urges, but I'm not doing a good job. God is trying to teach me independence by teaching me dependence on him and not on people. Because my life has shown me there is no security.

I find I'm weak emotionally. I still want so much to have someone. I get jealous of other people. They all have partners and family and friends, and I have no one. I used to feel like I'm this abject creature, that I don't fit anywhere, and that's why the thought of losing the disease used to be so frightening. But with the help of God that fear is going away.

Eileen Rand

Chapter 15

A short interview with Jeff Rand.

Eileen can be very caring, but she can also be very me oriented.

She'll take the attitude, "No one's going to tell me what to do," or "I'll show you and do it my way." She equates control to safety.

Background?

Sleeping Pills

Eileen's first hospitalization was in her teens. She tried to kill herself. Dad didn't know how to deal with it, and he was very callous. She was in Mission Bay hospital for a few days.

And there were a couple of stays in Mesa Vista. Anorexia is a cultural thing in Southern California.

Then she went to college, got her degree and went into Social Work. Her work was primarily with the elderly in La Jolla. This whole time she was running, dieting and restricting.

Then she got rigid with respect to not getting over 80 pounds in weight. Now she won't go over 70 pounds and has been sitting between 68 and 69 pounds. Joanne [the administrator at Cortland] was saying, "She'll do whatever she needs to do to pass blood work tests."

Eileen has been at Cortland Place from May, 2013 to the present, May, 2014.

Working backwards, I tried to find an assisted care home near me that would take Eileen's insurance. It didn't happen, which is how she came to be at Cortland.

From April, 2013 to May, 2013, she was homeless in Baltimore.

She was at Johns Hopkins, in Baltimore, from November, 2012 until March, 2013, when she was discharged for non-compliance.

Between October, 2012 and Eileen's move to Johns Hopkins she was at Rhode Island Hospital.

Prior to her hospitalization at Rhode Island, Eileen was in the Butler Hospital outpatient program. Mom was in Dementia Care, and Eileen was living with me.

[Jeff goes on to confirm a list of dates Eileen already has. What follows is Eileen's experience with Just People.]

At one point I wound up with Just People (for about two weeks), after which I had an apartment (like an efficiency room) provided by the owner of the same building.

"JUST" PEOPLE, Inc.

"Just" People, Inc. is a private not for profit agency that provides a wide variety of support services to adults with developmental disabilities (Downs, Autism, Aspergers, MMR and Learning Disabilities), people with Mental Illnesses and Head Injury. The program which was developed in the Fall of 1995, works with people who are considered "high-functioning", people who do not need bathing, feeding and dressing. Support services are provided in Metro Atlanta, serving people in Gwinnett, Fulton, Cobb and Dekalb County. The consumers the agency works with have the ability to live in an apartment without live-in staff but need staff available to them—some daily and some weekly and most with staff on property overnight that are available to them in emergencies.

Some consumers live in their family's homes but need living skill training before going into an apartment, as well as a social outlet with peers. The program which was the brain child of Becky Dowling is run like a family, after all her husband and both daughters work at "Just" People. Becky and Kevin live at the "Just" People Village in Roswell Georgia, an apartment complex that leases primarily to the population "Just" People serves, as well as overseeing the day to day services provided at Village Walk in Lilburn Georgia, a similar complex. To find out more about the varied services provided contact the "Just" People office located in Norcross, Georgia. 770-441-1188.[12]

[12]http://www.justpeople.org/

153

The apartment had a small fridge, a sink, a
bathroom and a bedroom. The unit was at the back
of the complex and they used it as an extra bedroom.
It was spooky and scary—but it did have a balcony.
At night when I couldn't sleep I'd go out on the
balcony and smoke. I loved the Georgia night-time,
especially the fireflies.

But, as I felt I had no place of my own in
which to live (that had mom) in it, I decided I was
going to die. I was getting colonics several times per
week and just eating an apple per day. To this day
Jeff is so angry about the colonics he would like to
get his hands on the people who were providing
them. He thinks the actions of these people were
nothing less than criminal.

Chapter 16

What follows are some free flowing memories from different times...

I never ever took responsibility for my actions. This is one of the things God is helping me with. I think he protected me. Because through those times, I don't think I was capable of taking responsibility. But I realized this morning that this disease is all my own construct. It's not anybody else's. It's in my own mind.

I blamed others. All those times I went to therapy and would end up crying because my dad was so mean to me. Hah! He put me through college. He loved me. He never had a father himself, and he didn't know how to be a father to a girl, but he did the very best he could. And he didn't abandon me.

My dad was such a good man, so I don't understand what happened when I tried to kill myself. Why would he try to force me back upstairs into my bedroom when I had a stomach full of pills? Unless it was the fact that I grew up with everything: a mansion, a pool, horses, anything I wanted, and I was screwing it up, just throwing it all away. I was telling him he wasn't a good enough provider. And dad had his own anger issues to begin with. So, that might be it.

155

When I look back I can see why he acted the way he did. But I still hold him responsible for his callousness, his berating me and the way he made fun of me on the way to the hospital and then just left me there. It was a perfect storm.

ભ

La Jolla Cliffs

The La Jolla Cave

My mom used to tell me I didn't have a sense of fear. The boys would jump off the 40 ft high La Jolla cliffs. At ages 14 to15 I jumped there with them, I chased cars with my horse and jumped over barbed wire fences while riding bare back. I was also a dare devil.

There's a place on Coast Walk called The Cove. Above The Cove there's a cliff called The Clam. If you jump off the cliff, beneath it is a cave called the La Jolla Cave. To get back up you have to swim down the coast about a mile, you have to climb the cliff or you have to swim into the cave to a dock and climb these old, wooden, pirate stairs up to The Cave Gift Shop. Most people would have to buy a ticket to get to see the cave. But not us. The owner used to get mad and try to charge us a dollar, but it never worked.

The part I love is I can remember going to the cliff, and there would be these groups of boys trying to talk each other into jumping, and here was this 14 year-old girl marching right past them and doing it. I felt like such a hot shot.

There was a bigger cliff that was 100 ft high, but I didn't do that one.

ରଛ

When I went to see the kinesiologist the other day, he said I was suffering from reverse polarity. He said that's why we're not getting the things we want right, because my body isn't telling us the truth. So he tested me and sure enough I was. He's put me on colloidal mineral Chi.

It's about truth. kinesiology is truth. And I thought where is the falsehood in my life? There are lots of areas in my life where I'm not telling the truth. I'm not telling Jackie about seeing this holistic practitioner. I realize that part of the reason my poles are reversed is because I'm not living in truth; I'm sick. There's a Bible passage that tells us that the truth will set you free. I keep asking God to help me with the truth. Because this disease denies my humanity. I'm not hungry and don't need food. That's a lie. It's not the truth. And I tell myself that I'm not human, that I'm not like other people, but that's not the truth. I say I have to exercise, I have to take these pills … No! You have everything you need when you have God. And that's the lesson. That's the truth.

I feel that I don't get what I need from conventional medicine; I'm afraid of modern medicine. Jeff and Jackie won't let me go to a holistic doctor because I've overdone it in the past. And when I mention it to them, they say that's not for you, you're going to go to a regular doctor. They say this even though they themselves believe in holistic medicine. So I have to keep it secret. This is a season in my life where I have to balance my needs—because it's my money. I'm an adult, and I can do what I wish. But they'll find out eventually. That's the truth.

CR

It was when I was back from running away and I became a Christian that I realized I was spinning my wheels and needed to complete my education, so I got my GED. I'd been running track and cross country all through High School, so I also joined track at Mesa, where I went to college. The major influence in my spiritual life at the time was Emma Lee and then she introduced me to Joyce Meyer.

158

Through fifteen international offices, we're working to meet needs all around the world. Here is an overview of the outreaches supported by the friends and partners of *Joyce Meyer Ministries*. **To date, our partners' generous contributions have allowed us to:**

- Translate Joyce's books into more than one hundred different languages
- Share the Word of God in more than 37 different countries through Joyce's conferences
- Broadcast the *Enjoying Everyday Life*® television and radio program in more than 60 different languages
- House, feed and educate over 1,100 orphaned children through nearly 40 children's homes
- Donate more than $11,400,000 to worldwide disaster relief efforts
- Feed more than 72,000 children living in more than 30 different countries on a daily basis
- Rescue women and children in nine countries from the horrors of human trafficking: United States, India, Ethiopia, Cambodia, Thailand, Bulgaria, Ukraine, Greece and Lesotho.
- Provide free medical care to hundreds of thousands each year through two fully funded hospitals, three medical clinics, eleven to twelve short-term

medical/dental outreaches and many medical partnerships. To date, we've been able to treat more than 1,000,000 patients worldwide.

- Distribute more than 2,400,000 hygiene gift bags to inmates in 2,900 prisons worldwide. To date, more than 118,000 inmates across 39 countries have accepted Christ into their lives.
- Reach thousands of children and families every year through our inner-city outreaches around the world. We're reaching the homeless, prostitutes, disadvantaged youth, addicts and the impoverished with vital help and restoration.
- Provide clean drinking water to families across India and in twenty other countries through wells and water tanks.

Hand of Hope is the missions arm of *Joyce Meyer Ministries*. Our goal is simply to help as many hurting people as we possibly can, to alleviate human suffering and to help Christians grow in their faith.[13]

[13]http://www.joycemeyer.org/HandOfHope/WhatWeAreDo ing/AtAGlance.aspx

Chapter 17

I have a strange relationship with my body.

I completed my GED while living at home. I went to Mesa College during my 19th to my 20th year, taking basic education and psychology. I joined the cross country running team. I wasn't quite as realized yet, but my life still revolved around eating, running and trying to go to the bathroom.

Mesa College

Our coach, Kurt Madden, was a marathoner. He had all of us go see a chiropractor. I began to see him and he got me on supplements. This guy was very good and had a great reputation around San Diego. His name was Dr. Berger. I was also seeing an holistic fellow.

Everyone was asking me why I was so extreme—in my running, in my eating and in taking supplements. I didn't have an answer for them, but it's rare that I ever feel a sense of peace in my skin.

161

There is no oneness in my body. My relationship with my body is that of a person communicating with an alien. It was nothing Dr. Berger did wrong: I abused supplements and exercise. I even joined the track team.

Marymount College

My dad was impressed with me graduating my two year college program. At that time dad was on his own spiritual quest. He asked where I'd like to go to school. We decided on Marymount, a Christian school, where you had your own apartment and a roommate.

We didn't get along, my roommate and I. She had a boyfriend who was over all the time, and when I was home on a weekend they would take my stuff. I, of course, exercised and had my rituals. I thought we were all really weird.

When I came home from school that summer, we decided I should go up there for a real semester. I chose not to live in the dorms again, and a woman rented me a room. I had a little Toyota to get around in. All should have been right with the world, but it wasn't. Everything I did was timed. Bathroom,

school, even meals. I'd be in the kitchen at exactly
four-thirty pm every day. My landlord couldn't
believe it. She would come in and watch me. It
creeped me out.

P.L.N University

After one semester I gave up and went home.
My dad suggested Point Loma Nazarene College,
now named P.L.N University. It was very strict.
Only Christian rock. No dancing, and the boys and
girls dorms were separate. I really loved the girls,
though. I was obviously screwed up but people were
very understanding. Becky Staniforth, British, was
so stable for age 19, and she had a great sense of
humour.

I never talked about my eating disorder but
everyone knew I had one. I'd get up at four am with
my coffee pot, drink my coffee, then run to the
washroom. This was a large, shared washroom with
cubicles and, invariably, someone would come in,
and I'd end up not being able to eliminate. This
would go on for weeks in a row. I was angry all the
time. To this day I don't understand my body, why I
have to have complete privacy and complete silence

to go to the bathroom. But if anyone else is around my stomach clenches and my colon shuts down.

I enjoyed college. It was wonderful except for this horrible albatross around my neck. Before anyone else began their day, mine would be half over—I shut down about four in the afternoon. I'd study during the day, because I couldn't think or stay awake in the evening. I only ate one meal per day at four-thirty.

Now, I must eat by five pm or I start to panic. I still get ready to shut down for the day at four pm.

ఌ

My reading for the day "Don't expect others who are not in the same place as you to understand you."

ఌ

The College was like Cortland, there was predictability, routine, and I felt safe. There were boundaries there, just like here.

I excelled. and the bulimia came to a halt. Then there was this guy Marvin. I met him through Sigma Fi Mu, the honour society. There was a Christmas party. He asked me out, and then he took me to all of these terrific restaurants and movies. I knew he was smitten, but I had no feelings for him.

Anyway, we went out to a party. When he brought me home, at the door of our mansion, he got down on one knee and proposed. I was stunned, because I thought I had done everything possible to discourage him. I even turned my head whenever he tried to kiss me, so that he would only get my cheek. Now, here he was looking at me like a puppy dog. I turned him down and said as much.

The next day he came to the side door where the kitchen was, and he asked to talk to my mom. He sat there and he cried and he talked to her and she calmed him down. He would come over a couple times a week to talk to her while I ran upstairs and pretended he wasn't there. Then one day my dad had a talk with him and he didn't come back.

Miramar

It was in my senior year. I was still on campus, was running and was using many rituals. My roommate was Myla Star Salmon. She was so out there. She would talk to the Lord all the time. Meanwhile Greg was flying F-14s at Miramar. He was in the Gulf War during the 1980's. He was doing carrier landings off one of the ships in the Persian Gulf. Jeff went to college in Boston. He had graduated with a music degree and was teaching. Mom and dad were looking at condos. A week before finals in 1987, dad had celebrated his 57th birthday. I was in chapel Wednesday morning before classes began, and they called me to the front of the chapel and said I was needed at home. Somehow, I knew my dad had died of a heart attack.

I drove home and mom grabbed me and began crying. But I didn't feel anything, and I pretended the behaviors I thought I should feel.

The funeral was huge. Just wall to wall people all week long. After the funeral I studied all weekend, then on Monday I went back to school and took my finals. I graduated with honours.

I know I've mentioned these things before, but I want to make a few comments: I think my eating disorder numbs me to a great many things. Also, I'm always in survival mode. And, finally, there's no room for people in this disease. In this last respect, I'm lucky to be a different kind of statistic— to have many people in my life. I just don't have a way to exterminate the disease.

After my finals, I began an internship at the Georgian Court across from Mesa Vista. It was a convalescent hospital. This was summertime after dad died. I was living with mom, and one day I took the Toyota in for an oil change. It's when I met Daroush.

He was an Iranian CPA student at San Diego State while working at the local garage. He asked me out. Unfortunately, mom was very prejudiced. No hard feelings, but those people needed to keep their place. One day I mentioned I was seeing Daroush and Mom forbade it. But she was too late; I was head over heels.

On the other side of things, Darouch was very traditional. He wouldn't sleep with me. He wanted me to tell mom we were still seeing each other. He didn't want to sneak around. But I wouldn't do it, and he left me. He said it wasn't going to work. Just like that. But I wasn't done. I had all these dreams from when I was young.

Fortunately, mom moved us into the condo at La Jolla, and I was put to work with the Alzheimer's patients and the crazy people. I was good at it and did very well there, except for the fact that I was unstable. So much so that I called in sick a lot.

For some reason, Mom and I decided it might help if we got me my own apartment. So, my Godmother introduced me to a lady, and I moved in with her. Pretty soon it was, "What the heck? I'm living with a Frankenstein character." It was after this I went to Remuda.

ଔ

One time there was a party of about 200 people. Mom had ordered two big boxes of petits fours but forgot about them. I found them in a cupboard and ate them all. I was still bulimic at the time. Such behaviors stayed with me until I was age 20. What finally stopped me was I was getting to the point where I couldn't vomit anymore, and I was too sick to exercise. I'd rather starve than have large amounts of food in my body.

ଔ

I had a stint in drug rehab as a teenager because I was an alcoholic and hooked on amphetamines. The group was called Freeway, but the whole thing turned out to be a scam, which my parents found out after a few months. While I was there I hooked up with an alcoholic. And the group leaders, Susan and Bob, were skinny, heroin addict, southern bumpkins. They were my therapists. What do I say after that?

Eileen Rand

Chapter 18

It's like sewage spilling out over everything.

I've become ill, and it's hard to know if
you've lost a lot of weight when you're constipated.
If I tell the administrator, she'll just say that if I'd eat
then I'd be able to go. But it doesn't work that way.
You just can't eat when you're like this. Whatever
you eat just comes right back up into your system
and floods it with all these toxins. It's like sewage
spilling out over everything. It's like things that
should have been filtered out are shooting up into
my body and it's making me ill.

CR

I just visited my doctor, and he says I have
parasites. If there had been any doubt in my mind,
it's gone; I've seen the worms when I go to the
bathroom. And there's so much irritation. Even
taking laxatives isn't working, because it's
increasing the irritation. He's taken me off of
everything and started me on this stuff call Clean
Start. It's got Bentonite clay in it, and I'm beginning
to think it's not helping the situation. Bentonite is
supposed to draw all the toxins to it and then flush

169

them out, but if your system is too weak to push
stuff out, it can just make things worse.

I feel like I have a big block in there, but I
can't get hold of my doctor because he's on a cruise.
And if I told the staff here what's wrong they would
send me back to a hospital. I don't want that to
happen. Would you?

When I was at John Hopkins, I wasn't allowed
a pen because I'd dig the stuff out. But this isn't
hard. It's soft, like my intestines have quit
contracting and won't push it through.

You know, one of the nurses took great
delight in telling me that one of the girls (this was at
Johns Hopkins) had a blockage and the bowel
movement was coming out of her mouth. And they
were all laughing at me.

One time I was in my room, and I was trying
to dig myself out, and it was in the trash can, and I
was waiting for the maid to come and pick up the
trash. But she said what's that smell and went and
got all the nurses and doctors, who then laughed at
me.

I used to beg my doctor to please give me an
operation and cut off the lower parts of my gut so
that things would just move on through.

I can remember drinking my coffee and
running to the bathroom and squishing my sides, all
for nothing. And all the stuff was just sitting in there,
making me sick.

The pain is excruciating. You can't stand and
you can't sit, and all you want to do is just scream.
It's a terrible feeling because you feel like you're
being held captive from the inside out.

Jackie says it's because I don't eat enough
Olive oil. Well screw you Jackie. It's the parasite
causing inflammation that's the problem. Is it any
wonder I'm like I am, when you can't go for months

at a time? I can't even sleep lying down. I have to sleep on a forty-five degree angle to keep stuff from coming back up. I have a big pillow to manage this.

There's so much contradiction in this disease: it's like someone coming at you with a knife, saying let me help you. I'm confused and feeling somewhat hopeless, because Jeff has said if I don't make it here they're done with me. It's a heavy burden to carry. If I wasn't a Christian, I wouldn't hesitate to do away with myself.

You know, because of the stuff I've gone through, I can't concentrate. I can't read a book. I do my little daily readings from the Bible and that's all I can stand.

What I do on weigh-in days (Fridays) is I put on layers of clothing and jewelry in my shoes. Then there are days where I physically can't do it. That's about a six pound difference. How do I explain that?

They think of me as a villain, like I'm always trying to get away with something. Even Jeff has labeled me as a manipulator, and says if I'm miserable, it's my own fault.

171

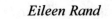
Eileen Rand

Chapter 19

I feel like a creature from another planet.

I did get some sleep this weekend (finally!). It's helping a lot to be seeing the chiropractor. When I saw her and told her about my pattern of sleeping until midnight no matter when I go to bed, whatever she did allowed me to sleep until two in the morning on Saturday.

173

And I watched *Gidget* last night, which made me think of Southern California. I was such a "Gidget" growing up. I still am a "Gidget."

CR

The book as it pertains to Anorexia? It's meant to provide a resource for people with eating disorders, for their families and for their caregivers as well. So many of these books glorify this disorder or descend into sensationalism. My goal is just to tell my story and show that the only thing that heals is love.

Every individual has their own road to recovery. Some never see recovery. I may never see recovery. Earlier, I recounted the story of a girl I knew who died at age twenty-two of a heart attack, which was a direct result of her battle with Anorexia. However, her life was best expressed by the fact that she gave her mom a chance to demonstrate unconditional love. Everyone told her to give up on her daughter (sound familiar), that she was a hopeless case. But Mary never gave up and when Cara died Mary had no regrets. She taught everyone around her that love never fails. And Cara sends her messages from heaven all the time, letting her know she's fine and that she completed her job on Earth while she was here.

Mary, by the way, is the one who introduced me to Clayton, the author who's helping me with this book and who has encouraged me to tell my story after mom died.

I'm far from well and may never recover, and I still feel like a non-human creature from another planet, or at least from *The Black Lagoon* or *The Island of Misfit Toys*. You get the idea. But God has allowed me to stick around, and all I know is that

love is the great healing balm. Mom exemplified
that. You can't bully or manipulate people into
wellness. But you can care for, love and support that
person and in so doing teach him or her how to love.
God gives us models like mom and Mary to
teach us and give us a tiny taste of what his
unconditional love his. You can't earn it. We get it
even when we're sick or dying. Pretty phenomenal,
right? Well, that's all she wrote so to speak. God is
pretty amazing. I love that he loves losers like me.

Eileen Rand

Chapter 20

It can't have been for naught.

When we moved into the La Jolla mansion, mom and dad spent all summer renovating, and I was left alone. That's when I got chubby, and being heavy at my school was unacceptable. That's where it all started.

Anorexia: There's no definition for Anorexia. The sort of biblical definition is *Loss of Appetite*. Anorexia Nervosa? *Nervous Loss of Appetite*. That's bullshit. When you're Anorexic you're hungry all the time. All I ever think about is food.

It's probably the most misdiagnosed, misunderstood, mistreated disease and it involves everything: the body, the mind and the spirit. And so many girls commit suicide, because they just can't stand the pain. It's a demon. It's a fucking demon.

The reason I'm writing this is it can't have been for naught. I have to believe that God has a purpose for me. You know, my mother gave a tremendous gift to me (by keeping me alive), and my family cuts her down, saying, "She enabled you. She screwed up your life."

This is why I'm so filled with hate right now: because my family, the people she was helping, have done nothing but kick me when I'm down. That's why mom protected me from them. And now I feel like I have no protection. I have no protection.

Because when I go to my brother's home, I am looked at like a specimen, and they treat me like I don't have any rights.

This is where it gets scary. Jeff thinks he's taking care of me. He's naïve. He's misinformed. Yet he thinks he knows better than me. He's also seen me almost kill myself several times.

Jeff accuses me of being stuck in the past, but I'm afraid he's the one who's stuck in the past. He's judging me by the same standards as when I was unable to think.

ᴄ⩔

[My name is Clayton Bye. I've been Eileen's recorder up until now. We've discussed it and have both decided the best way to finish the book is for me to participate via questions and comments meant to elicit some of the more difficult aspects of Eileen's disease. The reason for this is that Eileen and I have become fast friends, a happenstance that has seen me become part of the story. Note: My questions and comments will appear in Italics]

ᴄ⩔

Let's talk openly about your rituals and your exercising. For example, shortly after you arrived at Cortland, you were out for a run and collapsed. You may not be aware of this, but the home and Jeff and Jackie know about it, because of the policeman who helped you. Let's talk about the things you hide.

I walked out of the apartment to get something and Joanne came up to me and said, "Let's go."

I said, "What?"

178

"You haven't been weighed in three weeks, get on the scale."

"No, I've been ill, and I know my weight's down, and I've been dealing with this stomach issue."

"That's bullshit. I just talked to your brother and you're going to co-operate."

"No. You can't bully me."

"Fine. I'm going to call your brother."

So, I went into her office, and she called Jeff, and he said, "If you don't let her weigh you, I'm seeking guardianship. You don't get to say what's going on."

Then he hung up on me.

Joanne said, "You're a liar and you're a manipulator, and I don't care what happens to you." She also said, "I used to think I knew you, but now I know you for who you really are. You don't care about anyone but yourself." And then, "If you want to kill yourself then that's fine. Just don't expect anyone to pick up the pieces."

I said, "And you call yourself a Christian."

"That's right. I'm a better Christian than you'll ever be." Then she said, "Get out of my office. You're so full of shit."

Then I called Jeff on my own, and he said, "There's going to be a meeting."

My response was, "I don't know what that means."

ଔ

You know my life is so stressful. I don't get a minute to breathe. I never have a moment's peace!

ଔ

Anyway, I told Jeff I'd been dealing with stomach issues, and he said, "That's bullshit. That's not true."

He doesn't know. He doesn't know I'm not making this up. And it's like they want to put me in jail. He's probably going to take the car away. He's going to take over my money. I'll have nothing to say about anything. They're coming over this afternoon.

Do you think I'm a liar and a manipulator?

No, but I know you hide certain things, like how much you exercise.

Joanne knows. She says I run an hour and a half a day.

I'm not a liar and I'm not a manipulator.

There's something Jackie said this morning... She says you don't take responsibility for yourself. Maybe she's saying she's seeing narcissistic behaviors in you, the behaviors you're wrapping yourself in because of the intestinal problems.

Well, I really am alone...

Because you feel your family doesn't back you?

I feel like everyone makes judgements.

Yes...I could see that.

You judge me.

No. You asked me a question and I answered it. Narcissism is just a word. It describes a turning inward of our selves. I'm considered that way. And I think our disease(s) makes us that way. Don't you think so?

I think that people who suffer from chronic pain of any kind tend to be preoccupied with the way they feel.

Exactly. But people outside us see that as being self-involved. As being narcissistic. I don't know the word I'm searching for, but not taking

180

responsibility for ourselves is not it. Because I see you taking responsibility for yourself. You talk about it a lot.

I'm the only one responsible for myself, yeah.

And you talk about it: how you're seeking help through the Bible, how you're trying to keep things calm around yourself so that you can be better, how you're going to the chiropractor and doing what she says, and you're moving away from that other guy who was pumping you full of pills. I see that as taking responsibility for yourself, but your family doesn't see that because you're keeping it from them, right? I don't know if it would be something they'd see anyway.

No, if they knew what I was doing they would be pissed.

So I guess what happens is ... I want to make certain you understand that my job is not to judge you.

It doesn't matter if you do. You're going to judge. You're going to judge whatever.

I try not to judge people.

You know I really don't care. I don't care anymore. I don't care if you like me or don't like me.

That's just the hurt talking.

So, what did you want to work on today...

You wanted to be able to help people with this book. To do that we've got to talk about the things that hurt.

I'm talking about the pain of never, never, ever being accepted for who I am.

You've lived with this a long time, and I can see how people look at you as your disease rather than as yourself as an individual.

No one hears what I have to say. It's like I might as well not be speaking. It's like I'm an

181

Alzheimer's patient and nothing I say matters. They all know better, they all know what's good for me, what's better.

I told Jeff, "I know what I'm doing."

He said, "No, you don't."

He said, "You're completely incapable. You're completely incompetent."

He's sure bouncing back and forward, isn't he? One day he's fine; one day he's not. That must be hard to deal with.

There's no security. There's no peace. The only thing that feels stable is the exercise and the rituals. They're the only things that are stable. The vitamins are out of control: I don't know what to take and what not to take. I don't know what to eat and what not to eat. I can't sleep. The only thing I have control over are the rituals and the running. It's the one thing I know.

Mom's gone. I listen to the music every day and dream, dream, dream of what it was like when she was alive. You know, everything felt safe and predictable.

And there was peace and she loved me and she took care of me and she cared about what I thought. She took care to feed me the things I liked. Things that I enjoyed. She took me shopping. We shared things together that we loved—the music, we went to church together, we talked about things that mattered to us, and we listened to one another, we hugged each other, we held each other. I haven't been held since my mom got sick! I want someone to hold me. No one's loved me, no one has told me they love me, or kissed me or told me that I matter.

[Crying now]

That's got to be an awful feeling.

I feel like I'm already dead. And nothing I do
is right. I'm always causing problems. *[Takes a
break.]*
    I don't know if he wants to lock me up and
put me away—to protect me from myself.
    *I don't think it's a good sign at all that he's
threatening to take away your rights.*
    I told Joanne that I'm of sound mind. That
you can't do this to me.
    She said, "You aren't of sound mind, so if you
want to, go ahead and kill yourself. I don't care."
    Why do they think I'm trying to kill myself
when I'm just trying to make myself well?
    *I don't know why they think that. Because
Jackie didn't say that when I was talking to her this
morning. Do you think Joanne precipitated all this?*
    I'm sure she did.
    *There are some things I can say to you. One, I
feel like we've become friends. I'm sorry you don't
feel like I'm a friend today. But I think you'll realize
I am. I understand the importance of being held and
being loved and the whole business. I also
understand what it's like not to be. I told you my
wife and I don't get along anymore. She hasn't
hugged me in at least 6 months. It's been that long
since she's even touched me. So, I know what that's
like. The only closeness I get is from friends on the
internet and my brothers at my lodge. I get more
hugs from my brothers at the lodge than I get from
my wife. And I understand how lonely that makes
one feel. You, well you're isolated where you are,
and if your family is not giving you comfort, then it
must just be terrible. So I do understand. It's just
that it's not in my power to change that. It's like you
said the other day, I can't just blink and be there. I
wish I could. Because you are important and you do*

*matter to me. I may be too far away to do anything
to help today, but I do care."*

Thanks. There really wasn't anything to say
about the rituals. They exist to hold my life in place.

*And as long as you believe that the rituals will
stay there.*

They support me more than Jeff or Jackie do.

*Do you think your rituals are making you ill,
or do you think they're keeping you from being even
more sick?*

Oh, I know the running is killing me. It's too
much for me. I hate it.

But you can't stop.

I can't stop.

I go to bed every night and wake up every
morning and go through the bathroom rituals for two
hours. I wake up at four am. But I'm not ready to
begin the day until nine or nine-thirty am. It takes
me that long. I spend two hours trying to go to the
bathroom, then I leave here and go running at about
six-thirty am, and get back at about eight am, then I
do more exercises here on the floor, then I take a
shower. By the time I get out of the shower, it's
eight-thirty, then I fix my breakfast which is just a
green drink, and some fruit. And then I begin the
day, but usually I'm just so tired. So what I do is I
make whatever food I'm going to have for dinner
that night. Then I lay down until lunch time. At that
point I go get my food from the dining room. Then I
have the afternoon to work with you or run errands
or whatever. By four pm I'm ready to call it a day.
And that's my life.

*My day's quite similar. Without the exercise. I
start at four am in the morning, because that's when
I wake up. I take my morning pills, and I have
breakfast, and then I go back to bed, and if I'm
lucky, I sleep until six or six-thirty. Then I spend the*

184

morning with emails and writing. A lot of the time, now, it's listening to the tapes because it's too much for me to try and transcribe all at once. So I try to transcribe part of the tape on our off days, then the rest on the morning before we meet. By the time I'm done that I'm so tired I nap until it's time for our meeting. Then we'll put in our one to two hours, after which I must rest again. After my rest I'll run a few errands before I shut down the day by four pm. I quit at four because, most of the time, I just can't think any more.

Yeah.

The difference between you and I is I don't do the exercise, because I can't. That means I'm overweight and you're underweight. We make a fine pair.

That's funny, because many of my friends are overweight.

But, I want to earn my weight. And I know I can, because when I was feeling better, I was eating. In fact, I still enjoy my evening meal. Tonight I'm having Quiche and vegetables and a salad and a croissant and a little dessert.

That's awesome!

I always make a beautiful dinner. I try to duplicate what Mom and I did at home.

Well that's a nice ritual to have.

But Jeff wants to even take that away from me.

He wants you eating in the dining room.

Where I sit and I wait, anxious because I never get what I ordered or it's too little. Then you say, "You forgot to bring the tartar sauce or a pat of butter," and then you're sitting for another half an hour before they even bring it. Whereas if I forget the butter, my fridge is right there and I can grab it.

*Well, you know what? If I was in your
position, I'd be standing up to him, telling him to go
ahead, that you'll beat him at his own game.
Because if you're of sound mind, a judge won't take
your power away.*

That's right. I know that. I'm sharp of mind
enough to write a book.

That's right.

And the book is to stop this thing from
happening to people. Because you can't threaten or
punish people into getting well.

*You can't punish or threaten people into
anything. You can make them do it, but they're not
doing it because it will do them any good. It's just
like living in a bloody concentration camp.*

That's how I feel. And I get scared all the
time. I told Joanne, "You scare me."

And she said, mockingly, "You scare me! I'm
not falling for that bullshit." She said, "Everyone
loves me."

She sounded so ridiculous. She's a bully. She
called me a bully and a liar and a cheat.

Wow.

It's me all over, isn't it? I'm so full of evil
intent.

Yeah.

I get up in the morning thinking what evil can
I do today.

And she even told me "If you ever interfere
with other people's care here …"

I see something going on that isn't right, I'll
speak up and say this isn't right.

She said, "You have no right to interfere in
other people's business."

*That's not true. You know what I believe? If
you see an evil in this world and you let it go on, you
become part of the evil. Doesn't that make sense?*

Oh, yeah.

You know there's something Jackie did say this morning. And it might be part of the reason she's siding with Jeff. She says she doesn't necessarily believe it's your stomach that's the problem. She's worried that some of your organs are giving up. So she may have been acting out of worry. I don't know. I don't know what's she's like when she gets worried.

The thing is that the doctor just called me with the results of my blood test, and everything was normal. My sodium was a bit low.

You know what Joanne had the nerve to say to me?

She said … I went upstairs to the cafeteria to fill my water bottle. I do this every day so I know how much water I'm using, and so that I can make my coffee and stuff in the morning. And she said, "Oh, and also, I know you're drinking too much water, because your sodium is too low. You're flushing everything out with all that water you drink."

I was like Fuck You, you don't even know how much water I drink.

We just went over this on Wednesday. You're drinking the right amount. I think she's your real enemy.

She's dangerous. And they think I'm dangerous. I guess I'll be going to court.

Unless Jeff settles down.

Which means I'll be losing their support.

Yes, especially if you win.

Why wouldn't I?

I don't know.

I just wish … I feel like right now you are the one person I can trust."

Well, I hope so. I'm trying really hard.

They don't realize the more they push, the
more they drive the illness underground.

*I wish Jeff had kept his word and done what
he said he was going to do the other day—just back
off and support you. It has to have been Joanne. She
must have really laid into it. Because Jackie says
that whenever Jeff gets upset he gets so stressed he
gets to a point where he just blows up. And then he
comes back. So maybe, just maybe, he'll settle down
and come back into line again."*

Well the thing is they're so black and white.
It's like when I called him back. He treats me like I
don't matter.

He said, "We're done. Clearly you want to kill
yourself."

I said, "I'm dealing with stomach issues."

And he said, "No you're not."

Fuck you! You don't live in my body.

It's like if somebody had a migraine and you
said, "You don't have a headache. It's all in your
mind. You're making it up."

*And guess what? That's happened to me.
When they first were looking for a diagnosis for
what was wrong with me, I went to a blood
specialist. There's a marker for Rheumatoid
Arthritis and only 70 percent of people have it. I'm
one of the 30% who don't. Yet on that basis alone,
because I didn't have the marker, the doctor said,
"This is all in your head. I recommend you get to a
psychiatrist as soon as is possible. You need help."*

People like that need help.

*I'd say so. My wife was standing there too,
and we were both absolutely floored.*

Well, also, it's completely negating whatever
you're feeling and saying.

*You know, when I went to see them, I was like
an eighty year-old man so bent over I could hardly*

*even stand. I had to use a cane. My knees: every step
I took, it was like somebody was jabbing needles into
my knees. And then she tells me it's all in my head.*

Thank you so much. Anyway, the joy in my
life right now is working on this book and listening
to my music and eating my dinner. Those are the
three highlights of my life. *[laughs]*

I really do hate running. It's painful. There are
also times when I don't think I'm going to make it
back. And then I think—that's okay too.

That's a terrible thought.

It's really that my healing is up to God.
Maybe that's not taking responsibility, but I know
I've done everything in my power. I know this has
not been a choice. Do you think I choose to go
through this every day?

No.

I'm trying to be free.

*I don't know a lot about compulsions. But I do
know that people who have them can't control them.
It's almost like ... Well they call it OCD right.
Obsessive Compulsive Disorder.*

It's not OCD as much as it's just needing to
keep everything the same. Because everything just
feels like death. I mean one minute I can breathe and
now I can't breathe again.

Yeah.

And they ask what causes hiatus hernia?
Breathing. You know constantly breathing from
your chest because you're so frightened. She
laughed at me and she made fun of me.

"I'm scared," she said, "You big bully. You're
a liar, a manipulator. Nobody's scared of me. You're
the real bully."

I said, "Fuck you! You should hear the
residents talk."

Nobody likes her. She's a bully.

She sounds like one.

She is.

She says, "I help so many people. You don't want help. And that's fine by me."

You see, that's what you need Jeff and Jackie to be. You need them to be a buffer between her and you.

Well, she said she's done with me anyway. And I said, "Fine. See ya."

Good. Maybe that will be a good thing.

Yeah, but Jeff isn't going to be happy with that. And if she's done with me, why are we having a meeting?

Hmm ... So when is this meeting happening?

Oh you know Jeff, "I don't live by a schedule."

Chapter 21

Behemoth: a huge or monstrous creature

Would you be willing to talk to Jeff?
Absolutely. If you think it will do some good.
I mean, this afternoon when he comes. Would you mind talking to him?
Sure, but I don't know how Joanne would feel about me being involved.
I don't care what Joanne thinks.
Maybe you, I, Jeff and Jackie could talk.
That would be best.
Joanne can go and jump in a lake as far as I'm concerned.
I don't think there's a lake big enough to hold her. She's pretty big.
(I laugh)
I call her the behemoth. That old Biblical creature. In fact, if Joanne was an animal, she would be a T-Rex.
That's one of my favourite movies, by the way, Jurassic Park.
It's a fun movie, isn't it?
The other night I watched *Gidget*, which brought back so many old memories. I mean the original one, with Sandra Dee.

191

I don't watch much TV. If I want to watch something, I watch it on the computer on Netflix. I find that I get too tired for TV. I get halfway through a good show, and I just can't watch it any more.

One movie I can recommend that just came out is *Heaven is for Real*. You've got to see it. I'd read the book. It just kind of reaffirmed everything I believe in, you know?

It's about a boy who sees heaven, isn't it?

He died on the operating table, and while he was gone he went to heaven where he met Jesus and his relatives and stuff. He was only three or four, and he kept saying to his mom how come you never told me I had a baby sister? Apparently she had lost the child in utero and she didn't even know the sex. He told her it was a girl, and that he had met her. "She doesn't have a name because you didn't name her," he said. So they gave her a name. He also met his grandfather, and he told his dad things he couldn't possibly know. He said, "I met Pop Pop when I was in heaven."

That's funny. They called my grandfather, Grandpa Bang Bang, because every time a kid pulled on his finger he would go "Bang!"

Well, I do believe in all that, and I believe if I pray right now, I'll be able to talk to mom and dad. They know what to do.

I hope so.

I'll talk to God. He always knows.

Clayton, when you've lost all these fights and have been sent to a place like Johns Hopkins and have been kicked out onto the street by people who supposedly care about you, it's the most twisted, fucked-up care I ever saw. My mom was the only person on earth I ever met who knew how to give unconditional love. Her and Cara and Cara's mom, Mary.

192

℘

Eileen sings *You Raise Me Up* by Celtic Women.

℘

I used to sing that song to my mom.
You have a good voice.
I used to be the lead singer in a Rock 'n Roll band.
Yes, you were.
The book: you have the beginning, the middle and three quarters, and the end is now. How things are right now.
I had an idea. I'll run it by you. What I was thinking is that I've got these interviews with different people, and I thought if I interspersed them between the chapters of the past, it might add a little flavour.
I think the way we're working on this, it's very much a work in progress, and I think that's how it's going to end, it's never finished, you're never done. It isn't over until you're gone.
You know what I've realized? I've realized that ever since I was a little girl I learned to fear people. And the one person I didn't fear was my mom.
Maybe it's time to stop being afraid of people.
I'm afraid of people because they have the power to hurt. And they use that power too often.
I've gotten to a place where people don't hurt me anymore. I've taken on the attitude that life's far too short to be bothered by people who aren't pleasant to be around.
But Clayton, you're not being threatened with all your freedom being taken away from you.

193

No, the closest I came to that was when I was committed on Four North here (for severe depression).

"Four North. How many times have I been on Four North? When I went to UCLA, then when I was in Rhode Island Hospital, and then when I went to Baltimore I was on Four North."

Why do they do that?

Either it's a really strange coincidence or they do it for some reason.

Well, they do get sunlight morning, afternoon and evening.

ଔ

Jeff comes in.

"Hey Clayton."

"Hey Jeff."

"What's going on my friend."

"Well, you have your sister scared to death. We've been talking about it, and I don't know what's going on."

"Here's one for you: she's got the rest of the people in her life who love her scared to death."

"Yeah, I understand that. But she's trying to live her life. You see, my job with this book is to sit and listen, and I've listened to an awful lot of stuff. I see her every day trying to break this thing. And she's just scared to death that people are going— that you are going—to come in and take away the little power she has to do that.

I understand your concern about her weight and things, but ... I don't know what to say. I get the feeling that threatening and coming in forcefully is just the wrong approach. I feel it really strongly. And it's not because I'm manipulated or anything. I wouldn't be saying this if she hadn't asked me to. I don't want to interfere. But it's like she's asking me

*to champion for her. And if that's the case, I'd kind
of like to know what you're thinking. She said you're
threatening to take control, to have her made a
ward?"*

"Yes, I was considering that I should seek
guardianship, yeah."

"She doesn't respond well to threats."

"Yeah, that's pretty clear. If you say don't do
anything, that's her motivation to do it."

Eileen says, "That's not true."

"I'm having a conversation with Clayton."

She replies, "Yes, but do you remember what
we talked about? The more people try to move me
around, the more I want to stay in place?"

*"Yeah, that's exactly what she says. That's
what the running and the exercise and all those
other things are about. It's the only control she feels
she has. And she doesn't know how to get rid of
them. She's in a rough place."*

"All this is killing her."

"It may be. But perhaps she has that right."

"I have a hard time with that, man."

"I would too, but ... "

Eileen says, "People have been trying to
control me my whole life."

"No, Eileen. No, they haven't. People have
been trying to make a difference with you your
whole life. You don't let people in. That's what the
simple fact of the matter is."

She says, "I'm scared. And nobody believes
that."

"You're scared Eileen. But the fact is you use
fear to justify your behavior. You'll do things that
are in direct opposition to what people are doing
who are trying to support you. You say you feel
threatened by that."

"The only support I need is to be loved and accepted for who I am."

"It's hard to watch somebody who is taking active measures toward their demise."

"But you don't understand, Jeff, what really hurts me is when I tell you I'm in physical pain and you tell me 'Bullshit.'"

"Well how can somebody who is in physical pain exercise at the level you exercise?"

"I hate it. I dread it. I hate it, but it's the only thing that's solid in my life. My dinner at a certain hour, exercise at a certain hour. Jeff, it is."

"Jeff, I think what she's saying is that it's true for her. It may not be true for you, it may not be true for me, but the problems she's having with her stomach are very real to her. And, by the way, her Chiropractor agrees there is a real problem. If you want to talk to her, she'll back that up."

"I guess, Clayton, it comes down to there's not a whole hell of a lot anyone can do about this anymore."

"That's right."

Eileen says, "And that's okay."

"It's okay for you."

"God will heal me in his own time, and that's why I'm writing this book. This disease is so misunderstood. I had some measure of stability with mom, but all these ups and downs and threats ... I can't sleep at night. You and I had a falling out. You don't know what that does to me."

"Eileen, you haven't been sleeping before this."

"It doesn't make things any easier. Joanne was making fun of me. I'm scared of her. She called me a liar. She called me a manipulator."

"Eileen. Eileen. You called her a bully, you called her a manipulator, you called her a liar. So let's be clear about who said what, not that it really much matters. Presently, it's pretty clear that no one is going to be able to hold any kind of a difference with you. And everything's going to go the way it goes."

"You're writing me off."

"I'm not writing you off Eileen, I'm just coming to accept the fact that I'm going to lose my sister in the very near future."

"You're making black and white statements."

"Well, you tell me how it's going to go different. You tell me how you went from a considerably healthier weight—cause I don't know what you weigh—to way less than it was a couple of weeks ago at Easter."

"Because I feel sick."

"No. Look. I'm sorry, how is it that this magically started happening over the last two weeks?"

"I don't know."

And you have a medical opinion that you have some obstruction in your bowels?" Has a doctor said to you, we've taken x-rays and we've got clinical proof that demonstrates you have a problem?"

"I'd be happy to do that."

"Good, you should. You should get a medical opinion. Get yourself checked out to see if there's actually something going on."

"I know there's inflammation there."

"No, you're not a doctor."

"I know what I feel."

"Well sometimes you can get physical symptoms that you might mistake for something else. I don't know, I'm not a doctor."

"Jeff, the not eating came as a result of being unable to eat, because I felt sick."

197

"You know what, you don't have to justify it anymore. I'm coming to the place where I'm beginning to accept there's nothing that anybody can do to save you from yourself."

"Except love me. And accept me for who I am."

"There was a person that you used to be. There was a person in there once."

"And you don't see a person in there now?"

"What I see is somebody who's trapped by a disease."

"Clayton, do see a person or do you see a difference?"

"I see both. I see the disease and I see the person. Because I get to sit and listen to the person every day. What she's asking for must be really hard for you, Jeff, but I think she asked me to speak because I believe taking the control away from her is the absolute worst. I don't think it will save her. I really don't."

"I don't think it will either, Clayton."

"So just doing what she's asking, caring for her. You know she says nobody has hugged her in so long, she thinks it's almost since her mother died. She's not being treated like a person. She's being treated like a disease."

"You see, that's an incredible overstatement."

"Is it?"

"That is an incredible distortion of what's going on."

"Okay."

"She lives in a place where up until recently she's had friends here, and she was participating at family events."

"Well, tell Jeff what those events do to me, that they set me back for days."

"Well, Eileen, how did an event that was focused on relationships and family being together, how did that do something to you? How did you take action against yourself because of that?"

"There's so much food it overwhelms me."

"And Jeff, she spent the week after Easter trying to get rid of the food in her system. Which is part of the disease. I admit it."

"All I can say, Clayton, is having the opportunity to record this and communicate this way is some way of completing. And what I'm afraid of is this is like the suicide note."

"All I want to do is be free."

"And when do you plan to do that?"

"I've struggled with this bowel thing for so many years and nobody has taken me seriously."

"How many doctors have you been to that say there's nothing there?"

"It's not true. When I was at UCLA and when I was at Baltimore they told me …"

"Okay. What did medical doctors tell you."

"They gave me laxatives. I'm not going to spend the rest of my life on laxatives."

"You got to do what you've got to do. Here's a man who does what he has to do every day."

"And I'm trying to find ways to do this that aren't making me an invalid. I've been dependent on laxatives, and now my life revolves around having a bowel movement. I'm sick of it."

"Well, it seems like that is kind of what is driving you right now."

"I'm in a lot of pain, all of the time."

"Okay, well in a situation like that you work with medical doctors to help you get better. If you want to break out of this and be free, then you break out of this and be free. That's what you do. You take action that's consistent with being open and free."

"Part of that is doing what I'm doing. I'm working on this book and …"

"I think it's a wonderful thing."

"I agree with you about breaking free. I've talked to her about the running today, but she doesn't seem to have the power to break out of the running. You're worried about her dying? The running is probably the worst thing that's happening right now."

"Agreed, and maybe you can't stop it, but you can get it to a point …"

"I had it modified, but Easter threw me off, and I never caught my balance."

"Easter was a month ago."

"I know, and I never caught my balance."

"That's another phrase you use, Eileen, when you want to stay in your current behavior and justify that behavior, you say you've got to catch your balance. There's a series of things and phrases that you consistently use when you want to stay where you are and don't want to be interfered with. The interaction we had on Monday. That absolutely over the top reaction when I asked you about eating in the dining room. Why did you stop and ask me about that? The level of anger and rage that came out of you based on a couple of things. And you used to be part of this community just weeks ago, not some long period of time gone past.

"A couple of weeks ago was when my system completely shut down."

"Maybe there's something going on that you need to have looked after by a medical professional."

"She is looking into it."

"Great."

"I'll go for an x-ray, and take a picture."

"When's the next time you see your doctor?"

"In a couple of weeks."

"I'd make an appointment sooner."

"Who's your doctor."

"Dr. D ..."

"Then call her up and say I've got some stuff going on, and I need to see a doctor."

"I'll talk to her about it."

"Good."

"She took a blood test. She said everything is normal."

"Mhmm."

"She said there are signs of inflammation."

"Okay. I'd say if there's something persistent going on like this, I'd get it looked at and get it fixed."

"The other reason is that for people like me structure and predictability are very important."

"So, how is this not structured and what is unpredictable?"

"The reason I don't eat in the dining room anymore is that it's a very enclosing experience and it's cold, there's no music, and I wait and wait and wait to eat my food, and half the time when they bring it, it's not what I ordered or they've decided to cut back on the proportions, and if they forget something, which they invariably do, it's another half hour of waiting for them to bring it back. And I don't enjoy it; it's not comfortable for me. I can be comfortable here, warm in my room, watch TV, listen to my music, and be at peace. When I eat, I need to have peace. And when I'm in that dining room I don't have that. I feel like crying half the time."

"So here's my request Eileen: you're asking for consideration to be allowed to do what you need to do. I'm asking you to be communicative and considerate of the people who care about you. And recognize their frustration and sadness at seeing what's happening."

"But when I tell people what's happening with me they say I'm not telling the truth."

"Hear what I'm saying. You want to be heard; I'm asking you to hear me. You've got a woman across the hall, Joanne, who actually cares about you."

"She doesn't. And she told me she didn't."

"Try to listen to me. The fact that you can't see it doesn't mean that it's not true. She actually does care about you. She cares about your health and she cares about your well being. She actually likes you."

"She said I'm a liar, a manipulator and a bully."

"Eileen. She actually does care about you. People who don't care don't behave the way she behaves. Joanne is a caretaker, she's a nurse, okay? She's responsible for everybody in here. That's her job, and she takes it very seriously. When Joanne thinks there's an issue, she's going to do what she can to make a difference. And she's trying to make a difference with you."

"You want to take away my freedoms."

"She's gotten the message: don't try. So she's not."

"I want to be treated like a normal person."

"Well that's going to be hard. Because you're not acting like a normal person. Normal people who are sick want to be helped. You don't want to be helped."

"Can I make a suggestion, too, Eileen? Have you tried to get some anti-inflammatories?"

"Well that's what the doctor had me on, and I couldn't handle the side effects and the constipation that came with it."

"You were taking tablets? There are anti-inflammatories like I take that are needles. Things like Humira."

"All those things caused more pain and nausea and constipation, and the natural products are actually helping."

I understand where your brother's coming from, but I agree, being a sick person, I agree that you should have your choice regardless of the outcome. I'll give you an example. I'm overdosing on a number of drugs just so that I can walk. I've taken the choice that I'm going to have a nice life for as long as it lasts, because I am guaranteed, I am absolutely guaranteed a wheelchair, if not worse. So, I'm doing these things for myself so that I can have the kind of life I like before it basically ends on me. And I see you going through the same thing, Eileen. It may turn out wrong. It may turn out badly. But I think people should have the right to make those choices. That's all."

Jeff says, "I hear you. I don't like it but I hear you."

"I know she's not listening in certain aspects, but I'm trying to support her as best I can, and I know you are to. I guess it comes down to are you going to go to war with her or are you going to try and support what she's doing?"

"I'm going to try and support what she's doing."

"He doesn't understand, but I know there are ways to get well naturally. I'm sick of all this medicine making me sicker. And I'm sick of people not taking me seriously. Because I know there was a period of time a few months ago, where my body was actually functioning: I was eliminating, I was eating, I was enjoying things like French toast which I never eat, and I felt safe and comfortable. But

203

when my body shuts down like this, I'm terrified. People don't know what that's like—to have all that stuff just sit inside you and not come out. It's so uncomfortable. It's miserable to spend my days like this, just waiting for the time to lay down, because my stomach hurts."

"I see that you're pretty upset Jeff, and I'm sorry if I had a part in that."

"No, it's alright Clayton. We're good now, and I appreciate what you're doing for Eileen."

"Eileen, I think he means well. I really do. And I know you don't trust people, but if you want the family to support you, you're going to have to let them try to support you. That's my opinion."

"Then accept me for who I am, without conditions. Because I'm taking responsibility for myself, and I'm trying to find answers without burdening everybody with what goes on with me on a daily basis."

"Tough situation, isn't it? For both of you."

"Yeah."

"Before I die I just want a little peace, without having to go to a hospital and having things taken away from me. I lost my mother, I lost my cat, I lost my home. I lost so much, and I'm just starting to get a little bit of it back and this threat comes up again. I don't like it."

"I wish you could see how the ball has been in your court all this time, Eileen. That you could see that this is not some external threat. That this is all something where you have a say in the matter. I wish you could see that."

"Eileen. I think he's right, that you do have a say. He's listened to you here. And he's basically said he's not going to try and take away any of your rights. So, he is meeting you more than halfway."

"And I appreciate that. I just know I can get back to where I was feeling good—at Christmas. I was eating good, I'd put on some weight, the exercise was down."

"He just wants you back there, honey"

"I do too."

"I know that's what you're looking for. Anyway, I'm going to have to go. The one thing I'd like to say is when you guys are all done: Give her a big hug, eh? She needs it more than anything."

"Alright, man."

"Love you Clayton."

"Bye Bye."

Eileen Rand

Chapter 22

I was a frequent flyer

Awesome day: second day with no exercise, and I had a normal, unforced bowel movement that triggered itself. This is HUGE!

And it's all due to my new MD turned naturopath, who was able to target the systems that weren't working and conclude that I definitely had an intestinal parasite. He also gave me a schedule of small meals to begin with, so not to tax my system.

ର

"Dr. Strober ... My observations as a patient were that his approach was much more supportive and productive and life affirming than Johns Hopkins. Teaching positive self-esteem and replacing negative self-image with positives. Also providing supportive food choices, in that you allow the patient to have some control.

When you first go you aren't allowed to choose your food for the first week, because they want to expose you to different things, they want you to stretch your comfort zone. But as you become stronger physically and mentally they, little by little, would give more control.

207

So to make certain you understand, control isn't being taken away from you. You're just given a little break for awhile, which is important as for most anorexics or overeaters or bulimics your ability to choose becomes completely nullified. I can't describe it but you feel terrified at every corner and each decision is the wrong decision. So, to have someone make a definitive choice—like giving you two choices: one salmon and one chicken ...

"Well, I should have the salmon because it's better for me, but I really like the chicken. Except chicken might have MSG."

"Which do you like?" the dietician asks.

"I like chicken."

She says, "Okay, then chicken it is."

That was how it would happen. I was so muddled up with should and shouldn't. Don't want this, can't have that. And the dietician she would just narrow it down for me.

"Okay. Two choices."

Then I'd tell all the reasons why I couldn't have this and why I couldn't have that.

And she'd say, "Let me make it simple for you: What do you like?"

Well, I'd never thought of it that way. It was an approach that made all the difference. Instead of saying, "I'm serving you food and you aren't even going to know what it is until you get it." Then you have to eat all of it, like it or not. At UCLA, even when they did choose for us, they would say this week this is what's on the menu. Tell me the kind of things you do like, so when I pick for you, you'll enjoy it. They didn't turn eating into a punitive thing.

At Hopkins eating became a terrifying, punitive experience. How's that going to help me in my recovery?

It can't, can it?
The meals I had at UCLA are what I model
my meals after now. And I want you to tell Dr.
Strober that. When I sit down to a meal, when I
think about my meal plan or when Page and I plan
my meals, we're using the UCLA plan.

I found that program to be so supportive, so
nurturing, I believe that's why girls came back. They
loved the program and they wanted to get the same
support on the outside. If he wants to know why they
have "frequent flyers" it's because when we leave
the program, we're not getting the support you get in
the hospital.

My solution to this would be, and I talked to
Strober about it several times, instead of going
directly from the hospital to becoming an outpatient,
there needs to be a half way house. So when you
leave the nest—because UCLA is a nest for eight
little birds (on Four North)—you don't immediately
go into the outpatient program. It's too abrupt of a
change. UCLA did so much for me. But it was too
much to suddenly be out in the world again, faced
with my demons and having no recourse. At least at
UCLA when I exercised compulsively they knew I
was doing it. I denied it a lot of times but because of
the structure within the hospital I had more success
than I had failure. I'd go days without exercising.
Then other days I'd do poorly. Then other times I'd
do really badly for three days in a row. But having
them there and knowing I had their support, kept me
within safe boundaries. Then like a rubber band,
you're shot outside and that's all she wrote.

*If they did that halfway house, how long do
you think would be a good term?*
A year.
A year in a halfway house?
At least.

Doctor Strober said when he first started up his programs the adolescents he treated were on the ward for a year.

And now?

It all depends on insurance and money, unfortunately.

For difficult cases like myself, it wasn't uncommon for people to be there from four months to a year. The little girl from Canada was there for a year. I was there off and on over a two year period for four months at a time.

A typical stay for a girl who wasn't in crisis mode, who just needed some guidance to get back on track or to prevent her from going deeper into the disease, stayed for an average of one to two months. For somebody who was chronic or very ill or treatment resistant, four to six months was the time frame.

[Note: instead of expanding services, UCLA has recently reduced the adult eating disorder program to an outpatient service and has chosen to focus more on adolescents.]

Now, in California, there are halfway houses, but they're very expensive, and they really aren't that accessible.

I talked to Strober all the time about why can't we have a home, a halfway home. I even kidded with him and asked why we couldn't have a home for aging anorexics.

Imagine if I had the kind of support I need here at Cortland. My life would be so different. Instead I'm a salmon swimming upstream."

But guess what? You don't have a mystery illness anymore.

That's right. I have a parasite.

210

The place in Tustin, California was pretty bad; most of the girls there said it was horrible. But I've never experienced the diabolical treatment that I got at Johns Hopkins. The thing that kills me to this day is that Jeff defends them; I was the one who was in the wrong.

He probably defends them because you were dying and they brought you back to a liveable weight. It's just the way they did it was archaic.

And barbaric, and not only that, if it did anything, it made me even more afraid of food and my body. It's like all the positive re-enforcements I learned when at UCLA and Remuda were just wiped away.

211

Eileen Rand

Chapter 23

One week without running or smoking.

Gene *[the new doctor]* said because my adrenals
were shot they were craving stimulation, so he said
my brain was telling me I needed stimulation. That's
why when I don't run I want to smoke, because my
adrenals are missing the push and they're looking for
some form of stimulation. He said they're so dead
nothing is stimulating them.

Whatever he did to realign my energy I now
feel like I look. Prior to this when I talked with you I
was numb. Yeah, I felt like shit, but I was so numb
physically you could stick a pin in me, and I
wouldn't feel it. But now I feel I'm convalescing,
and I feel like I'm convalescing.

And I'm so hungry, I'm waking up in the
middle of the night starving. But my doctor is telling
me I can't eat a lot at one time. Today, I had my first
real meal. It was at lunch. But it's hard: I want to eat
everything in sight, yet I know if I do that I'll get
sick.

He said by the time I see him in a month
things should be good enough we'll be able to move
forward. I feel like I've really turned a corner, and
Jeff agreed to go with me to my next appointment.

CR

Jeff and I had a difficult talk today but a good
resolution. Mostly I just told him I felt like he didn't
see who I am, that he sees who I was, and he's
responding to that person. Also, he hasn't given me
credit for how far I've come. Then he explained
what it was like from his perspective.

He said, "It just seems like there's always
something with you. I get a phone call you've been
in an accident. Or you're sick.

I made mom a promise before she died that
I'd look after you. And I was sure I'd done that, but
now I just feel like it's never just okay with you. It's
always some crisis. And given where you've been,
it's hard to trust you."

I said, "I understand that. But you've got to
know I'm in a different place. I'm working with
someone I think is going to help me; I'm working on
a project I feel is worthwhile; and I'm actually
enjoying my life now. In addition, there are a lot of
things I'd like to do with my life, and I feel like now
there's hope for me to actually complete those
things."

I also told him how it is for me at holiday
gatherings.

He said, "Jackie and I totally get it. There's no
expectations; there's no pressure. We totally get it.
We just want you to know that the invitation is there
if you want it, but if you don't feel comfortable, we
accept that. I want you to come over when it works
for you, on your terms."

And I said, "I'd just like to hang out with you
sometime. Cause when we talk I feel you're just
talking at me or I'm complaining to you about
something. We're not really doing anything."

So, we had a good talk. Then both he and Jackie said they were really worried about my weight and wanted to get me on the scale.

I said, "No, you're going to put me in the hospital if I step on the scale."

But my therapist explained to me, "Eileen, it's like my work with some people who have drug addictions. If they don't let me drug test them for a baseline, then I feel like they're not playing the game, they're not co-operating."

So I said okay. And they all swore it would be strictly confidential. They weren't going to tell anybody. They just wanted a sign and to know that I'm working with this guy. So they weighed me and no one said anything, and they hugged me after. They all promised they weren't going to tell anybody and that I was safe.

But Jeff's coming back in 2 weeks and he says every time he comes he's going to weigh me. He says he's going to share the information with the nurse practitioner, to which I said okay, but to please explain the situation, that I've been dealing with these parasites. He was good with that and seemed to understand.

Did you tell them you weren't exercising?

Yes. They're proud of me; Jeff is just thrilled. Even the administrator here is pleased with me.

So you're getting support from everyone.

I feel it's well deserved.

It's deserved, because you're doing it all yourself.

And that makes all the difference. You see, Clayton, when these things happen, they do so when it's time for them to happen. I knew there was help out there for me, and I wasn't going to give up looking for it.

Now, I can't turn this into a be all to end all. It's just a means to an end. But I do feel I'm much more comfortable with this approach than I'd be with a medical doctor or to try and do it on my own. It's so scary for me to be playing around with these supplements I know nothing about trying to find an answer to my stomach problems. And now I feel I know what I'm on and it's manageable. I get up in the morning, I take a little packet of pills, and I drink this super food drink a couple times a day. I also take one acidophilus pill in the morning and a half a teaspoon of Fennel and Catnip before each meal. How much simpler can you get?

Yeah.

My stomach is still not good.

Are your bowels moving?

A tiny bit.

Well, that's better than nothing.

Yeah, I'm feeling ... even when I first started taking that super food drink, it wiped me out. Because if you haven't eaten for a while and you start eating ... I was just drinking a quarter of a cup, and it left me exhausted. I'd have to lie down. But it's getting better. I was so hungry today, I couldn't wait for lunch.

Cool.

But the other thing is I'm really, really disturbed about UCLA. *[reference to the scaling back of the adult eating disorder program.]*

I know, but that's out of your control.

The only thing I was thinking is Dr. Strober and Maureen are under this man named Dr. Patrick Strouse. And when I talked to Maureen, she said it wouldn't hurt to write a letter.

What I want to say was there's such an absolute need for treatment for adults and older adults who suffer from these things. UCLA had such

216

a wonderful and successful program and even if they can't be open, they should remain a model for other programs. Also it's important to show that besides the treatment program there's a need for an attached program like a halfway house.

If it makes you feel better, I think you should write that letter. One of the things I've done to help is I managed to get hold of Dr. Strober's secretary, and he promised to pass on our message and to have Dr. Strober call or give me an email. So, I'm optimistic I'll hear from him in the near future, and I can get the information for you to send that letter.

I think that one of the things I'd like to do in this book is...say something about this closure. Because the only other places I could recommend are Acute Care in Denver, Colorado (Short stays only) or Remuda Ranch or Page Love's business.

ACUTE Center for Eating Disorders

Comprehensive Medical Stabilization &

Expert Care for Eating Disorders

The ACUTE Center for Eating Disorders at the Denver Health Medical Center was founded in 2008 by the field's leading medical expert, Philip S. Mehler, MD, FACP, FAED, CEDS.

Located on a dedicated medical unit at Denver Health, ACUTE patients benefit from the extensive support of a major medical hospital while receiving care from a team of experienced professionals that specializes in providing lifesaving eating disorder treatment and conducting revolutionary eating disorder research.

Every patient that enters ACUTE receives a highly individualized treatment plan designed to achieve the following
- Alleviate any medical complications associated with severe anorexia nervosa or bulimia nervosa,
- Avoid and manage the potentially fatal risks of refeeding syndrome, and
- Prepare him/her for a smooth transition into a traditional inpatient or residential eating disorder treatment program.

ACUTE Center Highlights
- One-on-one care with a multidisciplinary team of providers
- Daily dietary and therapeutic support
- In-room patient assistant available as needed 24 hours a day, 7 days a week
- Brand-new, private patient rooms and bathrooms on a dedicated medical unit
- Comprehensive discharge planning and coordination of continued care[14]

But places like Shepherd-Pratt (If you don't finish your food they won't allow you to shower) and Johns Hopkins—when your mind is so messed up and your body is so depleted, you don't need more punishment on top of being completely wasted. You need to be treated like a baby bird. And it doesn't matter how old you are.

Jeff (we were talking about that yesterday) said, "Well, there was certainly a dynamic between you and mom that was keeping this going."

[14]http://www.denverhealth.org/medical-services/acute-eating-disorders

And he said, "I just think that the only place that ever made a dent with you was Johns Hopkins."

"They put the weight on me Jeff, but they tormented me and they put the fear of God about hospitals in me."

"Well, they broke the cycle. So, let's look at it. You haven't been in a hospital for a year. For you that's a big frickin' deal."

Because, usually, it was every four months I was in the hospital.

Well, he does have a point, and that's because you're frightened as hell to go into a hospital, right?

I'm terrified of doctors and hospitals.

So that's not necessarily a good thing.

I said, "It also made me less afraid to die, because I'd rather be dead than subjected to anything like what I went through, either in those hospitals or in the Rhode Island hospital."

I don't even know if Jeff heard that. There comes a point where people reach a saturation level. And that conversation yesterday? I think he was kind of saturated when we were done. He just took in what he could, you know?

Especially for a guy as closed down as he is.

You know, I think that's a defense mechanism. Because I think underneath all that, he's still Jeff. And he's still open. But I think he's in protection mode a lot with me. Because this last year was utter chaos with my mom and then me. And then I've moved six times in the last three years.

You have to realize he, too, lost his mom last year.

I think that she'd been ill for so long, that we'd already grieved for her.

He said, "I'll do whatever it takes to keep you alive, even if that means going against your will."

And I said, "I really don't want to stay alive if it means having all my rights taken away."

You know if it comes to that I'd rather live and die on my terms than have to live on someone else's terms."

But he also said, "There are times, too, when you're out of your head and I have to take over."

And he's right. There have been times when I've been completely out of my head. I mean, it must be really hard for him. He's trying to catch his balance too.

Well you know another thing, and I've got to be truthful with you: When Jackie came over on Sunday, she told me that in her talk with you, you said that these types of books often don't do much of anything. They don't even make a ripple.

I didn't say these types of book. I said any book. The average book now sells something like forty copies—certainly less than two hundred fifty copies. Hard to believe isn't it?

We'll sell far more than forty copies, but what I was referring to was that you had mentioned to her you were hoping this would create an income stream for you. I was saying I'd have to talk to you about that, because I don't want you going in hoping this will be an income stream—it's highly unlikely.

Oh, I never looked at it as that.

Then she misinformed me.

I think she misunderstood me. What I said was, I'm hoping that the book will provide a little success but mostly that it will have an impact in the eating disorder community.

We'll make sure that that happens. That I can do. I can't promise you tons of money and tons of sales, but we can make sure that what we do is target the communities you want to target. And you had mentioned some institutions as well. We can

220

also target those. I have no problem with that, and I feel we'll probably be successful. But these successes won't equate to money, which was the only thing I was trying to get across to her.

And Page is somebody who'll be able to tell you, there are certain online communities that cater to eating disorders, books about eating disorders, even poetry about eating disorders.

So, we need to find those.

There's a certain name, but I've forgotten it, but Page would know, and Maureen would know as well.

How should I phrase that?

Just let her know we want our message and our book posted on these eating disorder web pages. It has a weird name like *GoFish* or something like that. It's a weird name ... *Something fishy.*

The Something Fishy Website on Eating Disorders is one of the largest, oldest and most comprehensive web sites available on the topic. It not only includes a lot of valuable information on Anorexia, Bulimia, Binge Eating Disorder and Compulsive Overeating, but online peer support forums and a large treatment finder.[15]

◌

An interesting happened with this one girl on the unit when I was in UCLA. She was very, very bad off. They didn't think she was going to live. She was in her 20s or 30s. Her behavior was out of control. That can happen when you've been underweight for a very long time, and it can manifest in a number of ways. You can either become very

[15]http://www.something-fishy.com/

dead or you become like a wild animal. This little person with arms the size of twigs had terrible OCD, which is also a side effect of the anorexia. She would spend her mornings and her free time rearranging every single book and compulsively cleaning our sitting area. It was really sad to watch. Everything she did was compulsive. There were other girls with OCD, but she was really over the top. And I remember she would have screaming fits. She would hide food, and the nurse would say, "I saw you pull that butter out of your shorts." Her response would be to stand up and scream like a caveman. She would also run into other people's rooms and hide underneath the bed and scream and curse and yell at the nurses.

Dr. Strober went in her room some mornings, and she was always worse in the morning—which it is for a lot of us, you just don't want to be alive, you don't want to have to deal with your body or the food or even the loneliness. It can make you pissed off. So, anyway, he walked into her room one morning and she attacked him, hit him with her little fists, threw shoes at him, and he just ducked. He also kept approaching her. It was the only way to get through to her. After awhile they got to the point where they would allow her to be in her room and exercise compulsively for ten minutes in the morning, just to get it out of her system.

That's how he dealt with her. He didn't put her in restraints, and he didn't scold her but, rather, he let her get it out of her system *[sounds a lot like Gentle Teaching]*. He talked firmly and when he couldn't talk anymore, he would just leave.

CR

When you have an eating disorder you don't have relationships. A sign I'm getting better is I'm developing a relationship with my brother. I'm even developing a relationship with the administrator. I'm starting to wake up. It's not me through the eating disorder, it's the real me.

I do believe in holistic medicine. I just think it's going to take a long time to restore the imbalances in my body that were created by the disease.

One of the things I read in my bible study is, "I'm teaching you perfect poise and balance." Then, over the last couple of weeks, I realized I have been receiving lessons in poise and balance. Learning not to run ahead, because I always want to know what's going to happen next. Remember the scene in Indiana Jones where he had to take a leap of faith and step off the cliff, hoping the bridge was there, because he just couldn't see it? Well, God is saying, "Come on." Just like Abraham and his son Isaac. He had Isaac all strapped to the table and just as Abraham raised the knife God said, "Stop!" And Abraham goes, "Oh! I got it: God is telling me to trust that whatever comes next, he's got it covered."

I always thought that was an unfair test.

Well, Life isn't fair. And really, in some ways, having something like this is a compliment. Because God thinks I'm up to the task. And the fact that I've survived this is an absolute miracle and can't be for naught. That's why this book is so important. I really believe God has a message in this book. I don't want people to have to go through what Jeff and I have gone through. I want them to be able to know when they have this illness—just like someone who has cancer or diabetes—they can go to these specialty places like Cancer Centers of America. Those places work around the patient. The important thing is that you have cancer, they don't really worry about you having insurance. They'll work around that. They'll make it work for you, but still focus on treating the cancer. It's patient centered and it's adjunctive. You're part of the team.

Like this holistic doctor [Gene] I went to see on Friday: he told me, "Eileen I work at the VA, and a lot of the time when I go in there to discuss the case in the patient's room, the assigned doctor comes in and he's talking about the patient like he isn't there."

He said, "What I did one day, is I turned to the patient and said, 'John, what do you think?'"

"The doctor looked at me like, 'Why are you asking him?'"

And Gene said, "This is the person this is all about. It's not about you. It's not about your children. It's about John. You're not even asking John how he feels about the treatment or if he even wants the treatment. You're not asking him how it's working for him. You're telling him this is the treatment and this is how it's going to affect you. You're not asking him."

The medical model has just screwed things up so badly.

∞

You know what's amazing to me? The East coast and the West coast are like two different countries with respect to hospitals. I was in a medical hospital and a psychiatric hospital and an Eating Disorder Treatment Center in Atlanta. In Rhode Island, I was in a medical hospital and a day care program for eating disorders. I was also at Johns Hopkins for eating disorders. But I might as well have been on a different planet. Just being on this side of the country is like being on a different planet.

On the west coast, when I went to Scripps Green Hospital they were nutrition oriented: there was yoga, massage therapy, counseling, healthy food, nice doctors that actually talked with you, and a comfortable, modern and clean environment.

SCRIPPS GREEN HOSPITAL
10666 N. Torrey Pines Rd.
La Jolla, CA 92037
PHONE
858-554-9100

The hospitals on the East coast are archaic, dirty and scary—like something out of an old 1950s horror movie. Truly, I've never seen anything more barbaric. Even the assisted living programs were archaic.

We're so much further ahead on the West coast. Like the food—if I was living in an assisted living program like my aunt does? She's paying the same amount I do (three thousand dollars per month), and when I'd go up to visit her, we would eat lunch in the dining room. Our meals were beautiful, like gourmet food, with a gorgeous view of the ocean and a nice environment. Her room was more like an apartment, roomy and comfortable, with nice nurses and a dietician and a qualified nurse on duty.

These people in here (Cortland), they don't even know how to speak proper English.

On the West coast I was part of a team: there was me, mom, Dr. Schucter and Dr. Schwartz. And then it was me, Dr. Schucter and Dr. Hintz. I was even involved with my mom's care with her doctor. We were a team. And if my mom ran into trouble with me at home, she would call Dr. Schwartz. She was always on call, 24 hours per day for us.

When I was taking ECT, the team at Mesa Vista Hospital were always there for us. Those people were so kind. I mean it made ECT almost fun. I'd go in and see my friend the anaesthesiologist and Mary Lou, who would give me my shots and who would wake me up and give me a box of cereal after the ECT. I liked going under. Dave would always say, "Good night Eileen." And when I woke up Mary Lou and my Mom would always be there. I'd be happy all afternoon and I was tired. The only weird thing was I would taste the anaesthesia for days afterward.

ೞ

Any advice for the Anorexic and for the family member seeking help for that person? And what would your advice be for an angry or frustrated family member?

From Anorexic to Anorexic? Find somebody you trust. Ask them for their solemn promise that everything you tell them will be confidential and that

they won't use the information against you or
threaten you in any way.

Find someone you feel you can trust to tell
your absolutely most secret thoughts to, so as to
release yourself of that burden, and ask that person
to reaffirm their support and love for you even after
everything you've said, so that you can know that no
matter how weird or bizarre your behavior is they're
still with you. And remember, you can't have done
anything crazier than I have done. We've all done
weird or bizarre things, and the funny thing is that
weird and bizarre anorexic behaviors are no crazier
than what I see go on here (Cortland Place) every
day.

Know there's no such thing as a worn out
person. And, I repeat, I think the most important
thing is that you discover somebody you trust
enough to tell the truth to and ask them to reaffirm
their love and belief in you. This is so that you can
feel some aspect of normalcy. That you are a human
being no matter what.

I know at one point someone in my life said I
was nothing better than human garbage. I've never
forgotten that. I've had many people in my life tell
me I was nothing or that I didn't qualify for the
human race. Those negative messages can only be
relieved or overcome by unconditional positive
regard (a psychology term). And I'm not talking
about when you're dealing with the Taliban or serial
murders or people who have sociopathic diseases
where they have no conscience. But if there's any
single piece of a person that's reachable, you can
only reach that person with truth—not used against
them cruelly—but in a way that is non-judgemental
and helpful. For example, I came to you (Clayton)
and said, "You know I'm out there running an hour
and a half a day," and you said, "Wow." You didn't

judge me, you simply said, "Wow." Then you said, "What is there I can do to help." And I felt so helpless. But you allowed me the freedom of unburdening myself. You know there was a terrible ache in my heart because I felt like a liar. And now at least one person knows but didn't hang up on me or throw me out with the garbage.

I wouldn't do that.

You know that gave me confidence, and it convinced me to be truthful with my therapist and Jeff.

Then it gave them the confidence that since she trusted us with this information … you know one of the most important things I did yesterday was to let them weigh me."

That was huge!

They made a promise, and I made a promise. And it has given us a baseline to go forward with. Now we can watch it every two weeks, and hopefully it should increase, because I'm eating; and I'm not exercising; and I'm not taking any weird stuff; and I'm going through what my stomach is going through; and I'm being a champion about it. If I don't gain weight, we can talk about that, because I'll know that it's not because of anything I've done or not done. I'm even keeping a diary of what I put in my body.

You see, my doctor is worried about me developing refeeding syndrome.

Refeeding Syndrome can occur in anybody. They have this fellow they just rescued from the Taliban after five years of imprisonment. And he's in the hospital because he's going through refeeding syndrome. It happened to WWII POW's as well. They let them all out and many of them just died, because they fed them right away. What happens is it has to do with ATP and Phosphorous. Your body

228

uses these things to help with the contraction of muscles. So, when a person has been starving the body takes all that phosphorus and draws it to the stomach to digest food, because digestion takes up 75 percent of our body's resources. So, if there's no phosphorous available, it draws it out of the muscles, including your heart. That's why in a lot of people if you feed them too quickly, the phosphorous is drawn away instantaneously. So, you can eat a big dinner that night, wake up the next morning and have a heart attack. It's simple. When you get out of bed, your muscles are crying for phosphorous and it's not there and you're gone. You're just gone.

It's counter intuitive, but when I'd go to UCLA they would start me out on a diet. I'd get up in the morning, and I'd be allowed to have a bowl of cereal and some fruit. For lunch I might be allowed half a sandwich and a bowl of soup or some fruit. And at snack time, I'd be eating one little graham cracker with a little bit of peanut butter. At dinner I'd be allowed to have a chicken breast, some rice and a serving of vegetables. Meanwhile, I'd be looking at my girlfriends and they would be eating salads and cookies and bread and big portions, and I'd be going, "I'm starving!"

Then your metabolism starts working, and it's going, "Oh my gosh, I'm getting food," and you're just starving. I know the first week I was at UCLA I was demanding more food. And what they do is they check your phosphorus every day. You also drink a concoction called KPhos, which is a combination of Potassium and Phosphorous that tastes like Gatorade. You drink that three times a day. They also had me on large doses of magnesium because of my heart, which also helps with going to the bathroom. Then I'd see Lisa, the dietician.

229

Every two days she would say, "Well, Eileen, your phosphorous is doing okay. How are you handling the food?"

"Just fine. I'm starving."

"Well we're going to increase you by 200 calories."

So, I started out on 900 calories, and by the time I left UCLA, I was on 2,700 calories. And I was gaining weight.

The upsetting issue was that every time I went back to UCLA, it would take more and more calories for me to gain weight. Lisa explained to me, that every time—as an anorexic—if you gain weight and you leave the hospital and lose weight and come back to the hospital, you may have gained weight on 2,700 calories before, but now it was going to take 3,000 calories.

So what does it take you now, or do you know?

It was 4,000 calories the last time.

Holy Cow!

It's not uncommon.

But for me now, at my age, I'll probably level out somewhere about 2,500 to 3,000 calories. But, because of my history, I'll always have to eat a larger amount of food to maintain weight.

Now, though, I've got to be very careful not to overtax my digestive system.

ରେ

My perspective on the book now, is let's make this thing as useful as we can to other people, especially now the UCLA adult program is changing. The medical community needs to be educated. And there's so much ignorance out there. I just have to say as a sufferer, that not only from my

own case but in my observation of others—I mean
how tragic that a girl like Cara should die, having
experienced punishment for an illness that's no less
legitimate than cancer—this is a legitimate illness.
It's not something ... who would choose this? I ask
you: who would choose this?

I can't see anyone choosing it.

What really has burned me up, is when Jackie
says to me or anyone says to me, "It's all about
choices."

Fuck you bitch! I have so much anger toward
people like that. Righteous! Their self righteousness.
Fuck you! How dare you. Would you say that to
your friend with diabetes? It's all about choices.

I've heard people say that about diabetes.

That's bullshit.

Isn't it, though?

It's like if I said to you, "You can get up out
of that bed right now. It's all in your head. You're
just choosing to do this. Fuck you!"

I had a doctor say that to me remember?

I'm sure you did.

*A blood specialist told me it was all in my
head, that I needed to go see a psychiatrist.*

Well one thing, too, is I want you to let
Strober know I have found help through holistic
medicine rather than through the medical system.

I was talking to my Chiropractor this morning
about the good things that were happening, and she
said, "You know, Eileen, I hate to say it, because I
know I've said it before, but unfortunately once
you've been labeled a not normal person, people
don't even hear you after that."

Yeah.

Once you've been labeled—and that was my
message to Jeff in therapy—it was: you, you're not

even speaking to me. You're talking at me. You're talking to me like a parent to a child, you know?

I nodded my head.

I said, "You're taking the wrong approach."

And Chandler said, "What do you think of that?"

Jeff says, "I don't know. I don't know."

And I said, "Look Jeff, it's just that we need to get off this friggin' merry-go-round. You keep telling me I'm doing the same patterns, but did you ever stop to think you're approaching me with the same patterns. Maybe we need to change it up a little bit. You know, I just want to feel able to talk to you and not hide things from you."

"You know Eileen, it meant a lot to me that you called me from the doctor's office and said, 'Hey, you want to be let in?' I was thinking here you asked her to trust you and she's trusting you. So you've got to give her some space here. The guy seems to be helping. Because I definitely see a change in you Eileen."

And my therapist said, "There's been a shift."

"Absolutely."

"They call it a paradigm shift. I'm having a paradigm shift."

"Well, your body's having a paradigm shift. I think your body is driving this change. The whole idea that it's a parasite causing all this. That's something to get your mind around. It really is. Like these little bugs could cause you to run for an hour and a half."

"No, it wasn't the parasites."

"It was you responding to your body."

"No. The parasites were creating the weight loss. Because the exercise has always been there. The reason I exercise compulsively is that it's a way of numbing myself and getting rid of this anger. But it's also this craving for stimulation. And one of the underlying causes for these addictions is exhaustion. Adrenaline exhaustion. You're craving stimulation, because you've gotten this high at one point and you want to get to it again. But now you have to do more to get that high.

And I was so depressed because I'm living in this place with no sunshine, and I'm a California girl, and the only stimulus I felt I had was getting out there every day and running. Punishing myself.

You see your head is telling you one thing. It's saying I need, I need, I need, I need. You mean I'm not going to run? Give me a cigarette. They seem like opposite things, but they're both stimulating my adrenal glands. Also, I couldn't get my coffee strong enough. I was looking for stronger and stronger and stronger coffee, because it wasn't giving me any kick. But what I didn't know was I'd used up my body's supply of adrenaline. So, it's seeking stimulation because nothing's happening. That's a separate issue from the parasites."

I'd say so.

You couple that with what was going on— because I've run for years. Even at Christmas I was running. I was gaining weight because the parasites hadn't taken over at that point. But then there came a time where they took over, so my body wasn't able to keep up. And though I was eating, I was losing weight. Then I couldn't go to the bathroom. And I became so sick I couldn't eat. This was all followed by a toxic build-up in my body. And I was still running.

But now, hallelujah. some stuff is coming out. A little bit.

A little bit is better than nothing. And you have to remember you're only eating a little bit. And

*the parasites are probably taking some. So, at least,
has the mucous stopped?*
    Thank God, the mucous is gone.
That's a huge sign.
    But there's still a lot of irritation in there.
Well, I guess so, yeah.
    I mean it hurts, and after dinner at night ...
    Today at breakfast I had my green drink and
some fruit. And then for lunch I had the drink. It's a
super food drink: it's got like wheat germ and bee
pollen and all this crap in there. And spirulina and
Achia fruit and all this crazy stuff. Then I made a
wrap.
    This is so funny, too, because I was craving
everything in sight, so when I went to lunch to get
my tray, I ordered sweet potato, potatoes and gravy,
turkey, and egg salad, cause I didn't know what I
wanted. And yesterday I ordered tuna, two pieces of
chicken and all sorts of crazy stuff. So I came back
from errands, and I'm craving both tuna and sole. I
took a wrap, cut it in half, put in all of the chicken,
then added Dijon mustard, chihoula sauce, all my
veggies, sun dried tomatoes and then half tuna and
half humus and some nuts. Then I wrapped it up and
I had half an apple and my superfood drink, which
for me was pretty substantial. Because all I usually
have is the super food drink and a little salad.
    And I'm actually fine with it, because the
doctor said see how you feel. Well, this afternoon I
had my super food drink as a snack. Then, for
dinner, I'll have my salad with this homemade,
whole wheat dressing; and some turkey, vegetables
and a little piece of pumpkin pie I picked up at
Whole Foods.

◌

Again, I want this book to be a reference book for people. Even for people like Dr. Strober, Maureen, Chandler and Page. Why? It's been my observation that to achieve short term behavioral change you might be able to use punishment, but to achieve lasting change you need to be using a reward system. I told Maureen what my mind goes back to when I'm seeking reaffirmation is that she, Dr. Strober, Page, Chandler, Remuda Ranch and UCLA all had a positive, rewarding approach. A lot of places, just out of expedience, use behavioral modification. I've only experienced the negative in behavioral mod, not the positive, and I don't think there's any quid pro quo here. Lasting change can only be achieved through truth and love.

Peggy Claude-Pierre

Just like Peggy Claude-Pierre said in her book, *The Secret Language Of Eating Disorders*, that when she would sit with her daughter and her daughter would tell her this is what's going on in her head—my head's telling me this, my head's telling me that. Peggy wouldn't react and say, "Oh, stop thinking that. That's wrong. Don't think those thoughts. What's the matter with you?"

But she would say, "If I told you it was okay for me to eat this soup, would you agree with me?

"Yes."

"Wouldn't you think I was worthy of eating this soup?"

"Yes."

"Wouldn't you want me to have some soup?"

"Well yeah."

"What makes you any different? I want you to have the soup. Why don't you deserve that soup?"

"Well, I don't know. This voice in my head tells me."

"Well, that's the voice in your head. But you know just looking on the outside, like with the traffic light. It was green, but your head was telling you it was red, but you knew it was green. You asked me, mom is that traffic light green?"

"Yeah it's green, so you can go."

"But my head's saying it's red, so I can't go."

"Well, no, it's really green. You see it's green. Somewhere in there you know it's green. And I'm telling you it's green. Can you trust me on that?"

"Well, okay, I guess I'll take your word for it."

'Well, we'll go on trust for now until it becomes a belief, until you can be that person on your own. But right now you'll just have to take my word for it."

"So, let's have some soup."

Like with my own mom. I'd say, "You made this beautiful veal chop, but I can't eat it."

"Well, you can eat it. I made it for you."

"What about you?"|

"I'm going to have mine later, but why don't you have a bite with me now?"

236

"Yeah, I can have a bite right now."
It works, and you just do it until it becomes second nature.
Well installing a belief takes time. It takes effort.
You also have to know you're not fighting the person, you're fighting the disorder.
Yes. Well, I'm just talking about you or I. It takes time and it takes effort. And you can't just decide to change a belief. It doesn't exist in a vacuum. You've got to replace it with some other belief, and that takes time and effort.

This is where it comes down to meaning, just like I replaced the meaning of the disease with something positive and life affirming, like I'm finding meaning in my illness in writing this book. I'm finding meaning in my life, because I really want to help other people.

I was watching a documentary last night about St. Francis of Assisi. He came from a very wealthy family, yet he was unfulfilled and he was unhappy. He invited a friend when he went before a judge to give away all his worldly possessions. While there Assisi took off all of his clothes and was standing naked in the courtyard. His friend, brother Bernard, who was a wealthy man himself, and who later converted and became one of St. Francis followers, was terribly disturbed because here was this man who was to inherit all of his father's riches standing in the street naked, saying, "I'm so happy." He'd given away all his worldly goods, and he was happy. Brother Bernard was jealous. He was like, "I should think he's insane, but I'm jealous of this freak because he's happy!" Bernard went away and thought about that for a couple of weeks, and he realized he wasn't happy being the wealthy son of a diplomat. So he gave away his riches, too, and joined St. Francis.

St. Francis gave away everything, but he found meaning in his life, by serving other people and helping the lepers.

Serving other people is a powerful thing.

Like you can serve other people in a variety of ways, even in your own family.

But to make serving people your life—that's a huge decision.

Well, no, what I'm doing is ... I'm not going to strip like St. Francis and go down in the street to serve people. I'm serving other people by ultimately getting well. My brother and my sister-in-law don't want to have to worry about me, but they also want me to have a life.

Chapter 24

LuvnGodBless--------MissE

Hi Clayton!

Just got back from seeing Gene, the naturopath, with Jeff. Things are looking good. My intestines and stomach are functioning fine. My kidneys are still weak, though, due to repressed and held in anger issues. We talked about how the repressed anger is driving the exercise and the running and we discussed a number of ways to deal with it. I have an appointment for next Friday and will drive myself. It's fairly straightforward. My new exercise routine is a fifteen minute walk, three days in a row, with one day off, then three more days on, then one day off, and so on...and I know I can do it!

Jeff and I went to Panera for lunch, and I had my favourite! Then, at Cortland, we're having chicken pie for dinner! Nummers!

Jeff said he got your email and will respond. He's just very protective of me and doesn't want me to be taken advantage of, financially, but I reassured him he has no need to worry, you're legit. He says he thinks so too, but wants me to be realistic about my health, ability to travel, etc. He says he won't sanction a trip unless I get up to 70 pounds. Gene says we can do it and I believe I can, knowing that what I face is really buried anger and the exercise is my way of getting mad. I just need a better way to express it, and Gene and I worked out those details, which I'll tell you about when we Skype on Mon.

I hope you're having a nice weekend! I'm always so happy when I feel understood and like I understand, too. Yay!

LuvnGodBless--------MissE

Chapter 25

This is part of a letter I wrote to my cousin. I feel it says some important things...

"Buddy. Yay, So happy to hear from you. Wow. I had no idea what was going on in the real world. I've lived in a protective bubble for so long— all the hospitals, doctors and nurses, etc. This stuff is also so new that, frankly, it scares me. I feel so ill equipped but, of course, God is constantly on the side of weak people because that's where he shines the brightest. He loves the foolish things, (ie. me), to confound the worldly wise. Yay, I fit the bill of the weak and foolish ones."

She was asking what the book was about, so I said...

"The book is meant to provide hope, insight, understanding and resources for people who have eating disorders, for their families and for their care givers, as well. So many of these books glorify this disorder or sensationalise it. My aim is just to tell my story and show that the only thing that heals is love.

Every individual has their own road to recovery. Some never see recovery. I recount the story of a friend who died far too early, at the age of

22—taken by the effects of her war with anorexia.
However her life was a success because she gave her
mom a dear friend in my mom, their friendship made
while Cara and I were together at Remuda Ranch.
She also gave her mother a chance to demonstrate
unconditional love. Everyone told Mary to give up
on her daughter (Sound familiar?), because she was
a hopeless case. But she never gave up. And when
Cara died, Mary had no regrets. She taught everyone
around her that love never fails. Cara even sends her
messages from heaven on a regular basis: telling her
that she's fine and that she completed her job on
earth while she was here. And Mary, by the way, is
the one who introduced me to Clayton, the author
I'm working with and the one who has encouraged
me to tell my story after mom died.

I'm far from well and fully recovered, and I
still feel like a non-human creature from another
planet, or at least from The Black Lagoon or The
Island of Misfit Toys. You get the idea. But God has
allowed me to stick around and all I know is that
love is the great healing balm. Mom exemplified
that; You can't punish or threaten or manipulate
people into wellness, but you can love and support
that person and in so doing teach them to love
themselves and others. God gives us martyrs like
Mom and Mary to teach us and to give us tiny
examples of what his unconditional love is. You
can't earn it. We get it even when we're sick or
when we die. Pretty phenomenal, right?

Well, that all she wrote, so to speak. God is
pretty amazing. I'm in love with the love he has for
losers like me. Yay! Well, my bowels have moved, I
worked on the book this afternoon, and I'm talked
out. But it's just so wonderful to share with you.

Have a blessed evening and I so love you,
Your sister in Christ, Eileen

Do you have any idea where in the book you would like to place this letter?

No. It doesn't even have to go into the book. It just tells you what the book is about.

It gives me the understanding.

Right.

Well, it's funny you should mention it, because my idea for a topic for today was your definition of, understanding of and insights about anorexia.

Well ... that's ... that's it.

Eileen Rand

SUMMARY

*Well, we have another 30 to 40 hours of tapes,
but the story must end somewhere...*

Joyce Meyer, in her book *God is Not Mad at
You* states that, "We do not have to fear God's anger.
God loves you unconditionally. He's not angry or
even annoyed with you. God is to be feared with
reverential awe and respect. Not a sick, debilitating
and tormenting fear that destroys intimacy in a
relationship. God does love you, although he may be
angry with your ways. He never will stop loving
you.
 This is the crux of the message. If you receive
his love right in the midst of your imperfection it
will empower you to change your ways with his
help. Fear does not help us to make change. It may
provoke us to control our behavior for a time, but
unless we are changed inwardly we will never be
changed permanently. We will always revert to our
sin. In time of stress and weakness, if we receive
God's love while we are still sinners, our gratitude
for his mercy will make us want to please him rather
than to be afraid of him."
 Translated to human terms what happened in
my treatment was when I was at Johns Hopkins or
when my family expressed anger, I'd change my

behavior for a time, but the motivation was fear or for them just to leave me alone. The change couldn't be permanent because it wasn't done under my own steam. The things I remember and the things I retain and the things creating a change in me now are: First of all, that I'm beginning to experience God's love, which is allowing me to accept my imperfections, to accept the fact that I have this illness. And, second, instead of walking around in fear that I have a fault or something to feel guilty about, that I'm unlovable and unacceptable because I have an illness, I now recognize that these feelings only made me more afraid of people, or angry at people, and it made me sicker.

Going forward, I want to thank those people who have shown me unconditional love: my mom, Clayton Bye, some of my doctors and even my brother, Jeff.

I see that even though Jeff didn't consciously know what to do (and I think the reason he took more of a tough love approach with me was that he was coming from where he thought he should be and from what other people were telling him), in his heart of hearts, he chose the right thing. Because he wasn't loving or his actions weren't loving didn't matter, the ultimate result was he didn't leave me. He came and got me and brought me here (to Cortland Place in Rhode Island). And, in spite of the fact his wife didn't want me in their home, in spite of the fact that my other brother was saying she's never going to get better, in spite of the fact that Johns Hopkins said I wasn't a good risk, let her go, inside of Jeff was that core of unconditional love.

Even though he's still very unskilled in expressing it, Jeff doesn't always have to use words, and he doesn't always have to show how he feels, just the way I feel God's unconditional love now.

Jeff told me he sees the transformation in me. I told him, "Jeff, if you see any transformation in me it's all God's doing." And all I'm saying is that people are wrong. People are wrong if they believe that bullying or shaming or guilting or scaring someone into getting better is going to make them better. People are always going, "Don't you know you're going to break a bone?" Let me ask you this, "Do you really think that's going to make me better?"

I want to be well because I want to share some of the things I've been given. I want to be here long enough to pay it forward, the way people paid forward goodness to me. I'm finally getting this: that I don't have to perform. I don't even have to get well. Cara did nothing to earn her mother's love, and during her struggle everyone around her told her mother to give up on her, but her mother never gave up—and Cara died anyway. But that doesn't matter. In the universe, life doesn't end when you die. So, if I die tomorrow, Jeff and my mom will have been successful, because they loved me unconditionally. And that's how it works. They cared for me while I was here. That's all that matters. That's life. It doesn't matter how messy it is or if it never gets fixed. It just matters that we have that core of love.

And if it's foggy and it's ugly and we say things and do things that are hurtful, as long as you know that love is there, then there's no reason to feel afraid. There's no reason to be angry. There's no reason to continue to be sick. I want to be well to give back! I want to be well because I want Jeff to see me well before I leave the planet, whether or not I leave the planet before he does. I want Clayton to be proud of me. I want him to feel good about the work we did on this book. I want my doctors (Dr. Schwartz and Dr. Schucter) and all the people who gave a damn to be proud of me, and I want God to know that I had some tiny bit of enjoyment before I left the planet.

My current job is thanking people and letting them know I appreciate them … I remember what you said to me. I remember what you did … In fact, I spent this morning writing letters to thank people.

And one last thing I've been struggling to say in this book: I've been struggling to say that my mother was a saint, that she loved me. Whether some of it was selfish on her part or was enabling—I don't care. All that mattered was that I was loved and that she was loved.

Eileen Rand
Rhode Island
September 7, 2014

PART THREE

Additional Resources (in no particular order)

Eileen Rand

UCLA
Adult Eating Disorder Treatment Program

Partial Hospitalization
The Partial Hospitalization Program provides services five days a week for 8-10 hours per day (Monday and Thursday 8:00 a.m. to 4:00 p.m.; Tuesday, Wednesday and Friday 8:00 a.m. to 6:00 p.m.). Patients in the program are expected to attend the program on a daily basis. The partial hospitalization therapeutic milieu is designed to help patients continue the work started during the inpatient stay, with an increased emphasis on strengthening relapse prevention skills and strategies. Patients gradually take on increased responsibility for self-care, and are supported as they transition back to their home, school and/or work environments.

- Learn more about the structured eating program implemented during partial hospitalization.
- Learn more about the therapy modalities utilized during partial hospitalization.

Outpatient Eating Disorder Services
We can also provide referrals for outpatient individual psychotherapy or medication management for patients with eating disorders; Dr. Michael Strober and Dr. S.E. Specter are available to provide an outpatient evaluation and treatment recommendations. Dr. Strober can be reached at (310) 825-5730 or via email at mstrober@mednet.ucla.edu, and Dr. Specter can be reached at (310) 267-1495 or via email atsspecter@mednet.ucla.edu

For Healthcare Professionals
To refer a patient to the Adult Eating Disorders Partial Hospitalization Program, please contact our Program Manager, Judy Toy RN, at (310) 983-3274.

To refer a patient to the adolescent track of our eating disorders program (inpatient or partial hospital level of care), please contact Dr. Michael Strober at (310) 825-5730.

Mary Ellen Trunko, MD
Medical Director UCSD
Eating Disorder Adult Programs

**Science in the Service of Improving
the Treatments for Eating Disorders**

There is a growing understanding of how powerful brain processes contribute to behaviors that create and sustain anorexia and bulimia nervosa. Such knowledge has resulted in court rulings, such as a recent New Jersey case, that have classified eating disorders as a biologically based brain disorder. In turn, this has compelled insurance companies to cover eating disorders in the same way they pay for physical illnesses. However, relatively little has been done to apply new understanding of biology to develop more effective treatment. The ED program at UCSD is an international leader in employing new treatments based on science and research into the neurobiology of AN and BN. The following are examples of how we are using this new knowledge to provide better treatment for you:

- The relapse rate in AN and BN is very high, because people are often unable to deal with the reduced structure after discharge from inpatient or residential programs. Families may not have developed effective supportive strategies to maintain the gains made in inpatient treatment , and help the patient cope with stress.. **Our primary goal is to prevent relapse** by helping individuals with eating disorders, and their families, learn to be successful in a "real-world" environment.
- The fees charged by our program are mainly used to support our highly talented, full-time, faculty and staff who have advanced degrees (MD, PhD,

etc.) and many years of experience. Patients and families often have some choice in where they seek healthcare. Those who value the incorporation of new science into treatment, and prioritize the skill of the staff over the looks of the facility, will find our philosophy most appropriate to their needs.

- We use treatments derived from evidence-based or best-practice methods supported by the scientific literature. Moreover, we seek to deliver lower cost treatments, in the least restrictive setting.

- Our program helps people **develop more effective strategies to cope** with the altered appetite, reward, anxiety, obsessionality, and impulse control alterations that contribute to a vulnerability to develop an ED and the difficulties in sustaining recovery.

Contact us:

Intake Department

Toll Free: (855) 824-3050
Fax: (858) 534-6727
Email: edintake@ucsd.edu

Main Office - San Diego, CA

Mailing Address:

University of California, San Diego
Department of Psychiatry
Eating Disorders Center for Treatment and Research
4510 Executive Drive, Suite 315
San Diego, CA 92121
Tel:(858) 534-8019
Fax:(858) 534-6727

Sharp Mesa Vista, part of the Sharp Metropolitan Medical Campus, is the most comprehensive mental health hospital in San Diego. With one hundred forty-nine beds, the hospital offers programs for seniors, adults, adolescents and children.

Treatment Philosophy
Our staff is committed to providing dignified care and treatment to individuals who struggle with mental illness and substance abuse. Our Philosophy of Care is to restore the patient to optimal

255

functioning in the shortest amount of time and in the most comfortable environment possible.

We have a staff of more than forty psychiatrists and one hundred fifty health professionals. We understand that it's common for people with mental illness to experience stigma and barriers to social integration. We are committed to eliminating stigma and to promoting the fullest recovery for each individual.

Sharp Mesa Vista Hospital's programs and services include:

Adult treatment programs for issues such as mood disorders and PTSD

Arts-for-healing program for improving the emotional and spiritual health of patients

Child and adolescent programs, including treatment for emotional and behavioral problems

Older adult treatment programs for issues such as anxiety disorder, depression and phobias

Outpatient treatment program for opiate dependence

Residential chemical dependency treatment program

State-of-the-art chemical dependency recovery treatment

Transitional Age Youth (TAY) Program for young adults, ages 18 to 25, with severe mental illness

Treatment for eating disorders

Give
Your donations and gifts help us continue to offer a wide range of services to all levels of the community. Make a donation to Sharp HealthCare.

Internships and Fellowships
Get information about our predoctoral internships and postdoctoral fellowships.

Community Health Needs Assessment
Learn about and view the Sharp Mesa Vista Hospital two thousand and thirteen Community Health Needs Assessment.

For More Information
Get answers to frequently asked questions and information about Sharp Mesa Vista Hospital hours and calling a patient. Also meet Sharp Mesa Vista's chief medical officer.
To learn more Sharp Mesa Vista's programs and services, please call 1-800-82-SHARP (1-800-827-4277). To contact Sharp Mesa Vista directly, please call 858-836-8434 or 1-800-696-6899

Eileen Rand

In her role as Eating recovery Venter's clinical director of adult inpatient and residential services and associate chief clinical officer, Dr. Pikus is tasked with overseeing the delivery of clinical care by a team of skilled therapists providing individual, family and group therapy to adult eating disordered patients at the Center's Behavioral Hospital for Adults. Additionally, she collaborates with Craig Johnson, PhD, FAED, CEDS chief clinical officer, in the development of clinical treatment approaches and policies, and consults with the multidisciplinary treatment team regarding patient care issues.

Dr. Pikus brings more than 17 years of eating disorders treatment experience, working with adults, adolescents and children at multiple levels of care to her position at Eating Recovery Center. Previously, she served as associate director of the UCLA Eating Disorders Program, where she was responsible for program development and coordination and oversight for multidisciplinary clinical teams in the program's inpatient and partial hospitalization levels of care. Additionally, Dr. Pikus co-founded the UCLA Campus-wide Eating Disorders Partnership to promote collaboration across the departments on campus providing treatment to students with eating disorders.

Call: 1-877-825-8584 or visit...
http://www.eatingrecoverycenter.com/

Eileen Rand

Kris Shock,CPS
Certified Recovery Coach
Founder/Executive Director of SOAR- Supporting
Others Achieve Recovery, Inc.
www.soargeorgia.com
kris@soargeorgia.com or 678-480-4275

**Founder, Executive Director and Director of The
Phoenix House**
Mission: To provide opportunities for those in
recovery from an eating disorder to encourage,
support and uplift those currently suffering from an
eating disorder.
http://www.soargeorgia.com
Vision: A community of support for those suffering
from eating disorders while providing a healthy, safe
forum for those in recovery to give back.

Dr. Susan Schucter
Office: 4060 Fourth Ave, Ste 505, San Diego, CA
Phone: 619-298-1318
On medical staff at: Scripps Mercy Hospital

Eileen Rand

[From an interview with Page Love]

Page Love, MS RD, CSSD, LD

Nutrifit Sport Therapy, Inc.
www.nutrifitga.com
Nutrilove@gmail.com
1117 Perimeter Center West, Suite W-507,
Atlanta,GA 30338
Phone 770-395-7331
Fax 770-395-7332

Page Love, MS, RD, LD is a leading nutrition expert and owner of Nutrifit Sport Therapy, Inc., a company dedicated to helping clients reach wellness goals. The Nutrifit team specializes in counseling for disease prevention, weight management, sport nutrition, eating disorders nutrition therapy, and more. As a sports nutrition expert, Page has worked with professionals, collegiate teams, and individual athletes. Recent clients include the Atlanta Braves, the U.S Tennis Association, Men's and Women's

ATP & WTA Professional Tennis Tours, and U.S Figure Skating Association. She provides individual and group counseling for disordered eating and also works with programs such as the National Eating Disorders Association, Eating Disorders Information Network, and The Renfrew Center, Eating Recovery Center and the Atlanta Center for Eating Disorders. Page serves as a board member for EDIN. She has published a 35 module *Disordered Eating and Exercise* workbook available through her website at nutrifitga.com or through the Gurze catalog on line at bulimia.com. She has been featured in *People* magazine, *Men's Health, Tennis* magazine, and *CNN Headline News*. Locally, Page also coordinates facilitation of a free eating disorder support group on Saturday mornings called ANAD and a once per month breakfast meal support group called the Breakfast Club.

❧

Hi Page. Can you tell me about your program in a way that will provide useful information for anorexics seeking help?

Developed by Page Love, MS, RD, CSSD, LD. © Nutrifit, Sport, Therapy, Inc. ☐ www.nutrifitga.com

Page Love's Disordered Eating and Exercise Resource Handout Kit

Here are the disordered eating and exercise handouts the package contains (Contact Page for further information):

  --Activity/Movement Journal
  --Body Image and Self Esteem Worksheet:

Positive Self-Talk
--Carbohydrate Fears
--Choosing and Enjoying Foods
--Compulsive Exercise: Risks and Recovery Goals   X
--Considerations for Returning to
--Exercise
--Controlling Behaviors   X
--Dealing with Food, Weight and Body Image   X
--Dealing with Nutrition, Image
and Exercise Obsession
--Decreasing Your Obsessions: Nutrition and   X
Movement Goals
--Dining-out Fears   X
--Dining-out Tips
--Eating Desserts   X
--Evaluating the Nutritional
Adequacy of Your Eating Style
--Fat Fears
--Food Mood Activity   X
Journal
--Healthy Menu Planning
--How Are You Doing on Your Nutritional   X
Recovery?
--How Are You Doing with Your   X
Activity/Movement Plan?
--How to Fight Back Puzzling
Diet Fads
--Meat Alternatives & Vegetarian Proteins   X
--Mindful Eating   X
--Protein Fears: Are you meeting
your protein needs?
--Red Meat: Why is it Good For
You?
--Scaled? Try These Tips to *Kick the Scale*   X
--Split Journaling worksheet   X
--Stop Body Judgment

Eileen Rand

--Struggle with Counting?	X
--Top Ten Reasons Not to Weigh Yourself	X
--Top Ten Tips to Help Control Your Compulsive Exercise	X
--Top Ten Ways to Increase Calcium	X
--Ways to Curb Overeating	
--Ways to Decrease Binging/Purging	X
--For the Practitioner: Nutrition Assessment of Disordered Eating Questionnaire	X

ॐ

ANAD
(ASSOCIATION FOR ANOREXIA NERVOSA AND ASSOCIATED DISORDERS)
EATING DISORDERS SUPPORT GROUP

A support group for women and men struggling with anorexia, bulimia, and compulsive overeating as well as families and friends wishing to be involved in the recovery process

The purpose of this group is to provide the opportunity to:
☐ *Meet with others who share similar problems and receive support*
☐ *Learn and maintain healthy coping skills*
☐ *Identify and express emotions*
☐ *Develop interpersonal skills and address relationship issues*
☐ *Identify role of healthy body image and food in development*
☐ *Receive referral information for treatment*

This group is co-facilitated by a registered dietitian and a counselor who specialize in the treatment of disordered eating.
For more information, contact:
Page Love, RD at 770-395-7331.
St. Luke's Presbyterian Church
Room 212
1978 Mt. Vernon Rd
Atlanta, GA 30338
(Or see full layout for ANAD at the end of the book)

ଔ

Stop yo-yo dieting and the binge-purge cycle.

Vast experience lets us deal caringly and effectively with disordered eating, food obsessions and fears, and related health issues…we're here to help.

Nutrition counseling for:
Anorexia
Bulimia
binge eating
compulsive overeating

Nutritherapy sessions are offered individually or in a group setting and provide practical tips and techniques that are immediately useful. We focus on each individual's specific needs and work to improve energy levels, raise metabolism, meet essential nutrient needs, and decrease food obsessions.

Learn to get in touch with emotional eating and hunger using a "non-diet" approach.

Past and current clients include:
- ANAD: National Association of Anorexia Nervosa and Associated Disorders
- Atlanta Center for Eating Disorders
- Eating Disorders Information Network
- The Renfrew Center
- SAFE Recovery Systems
- Summit Ridge Center for Psychiatry

-I have served as the head dietitian for the Atlanta Center for Eating Disorders since 1995, developed their nutrition program and lead their main nutrition group (this would be similar to the outpatient programming Eileen most recently did after her last long term residential care in California, website: eatingdisorders.cc.

-I serve as the board chair for Eating Disorders Information Network, a non-profit charity organization based in Atlanta that focuses on outreach and prevention. We have developed programs that help with early education in schools to prevent eating disorders and help families better communicate with their sons and daughters about food, body, and weight healthfully...LULA, MOD SQUAD, WHAT"S EATING KATIE and FULL MOUSE, EMPTY MOUSE. Go to: myedin.org for more information.

-See additionally case **testimonials** regarding our work with eating disorder clients: Nikki Bennett, a former Nutrifit client, wrote this informative article about Nutrifit Sport Therapy, Inc. for her school newspaper...

Weighting on the World to Change:
Today's teens battle
to overcome eating disorders
by Nikki Bennett

Emily* was eleven years old when she began considering a process of binging and purging that would haunt her until age fifteen. "I saw magazine covers and knew I couldn't compare to the thin, blonde beautiful girls," she says, "My brothers were also wrestlers-constantly cutting weight and both my parents were on strict diets. I got the guilt trip every time I ate something against their diet." At age thirteen, Emily turned to bulimia as a way to control her eating habits and punish herself for eating foods outside of healthy standards. "I hated myself for not being able to compare to others, so I guess I felt that I could control my weight," she says. Her brother informed her family of her newfound eating habits and she was immediately put into counseling. At the end of the eighth grade, Emily stopped seeing her counselor but has since gone back to counseling for issues outside of her perception of food and body. She has grown, acquiring a new outlook on self image and strives to love the person she has become. "Punishing yourself for eating is different than being responsible for what you eat," Emily says, "If you don't love yourself, there's really no way to love anyone else."

Junior Scott Imm also knows the pressures young people can face to maintain a certain acceptable weight. "When you enter high school, your social status is defined by the people who you hang out with and you try to fit in with that group," Scott says. Like many young people, Scott began to view himself differently as he progressed from middle school to high school and also perceived his

269

diet differently. "It was a few years ago that I started to be self conscious about my weight," Scott says, "and I started skipping some meals and eating less which left me feeling weak and tired." Now at a healthy weight, Scott blames his past struggles with self image on the way that American culture devalues hard work, promotes immediate success, and glorifies careers in acting and modeling. "Young people idolize celebrities and the way that person eats, acts, and dresses," Scott says.

    At Nutrifit Sport Therapy, counselors and nutrition experts work with people of all ages who struggle with overcoming an eating disorder and/or unhealthy eating habits. "There is less fear if we present these topics in an open forum manner, helping to cultivate young people to ask questions and better understand what their bodies need," resident nutritionist at Nutrifit Sport Therapy Page Love says. Love helps teens, and adults, to define "normal" eating, which serves as an obstacle for many people who tend to overeat or undereat. "As stated by Ellyn Satter, normal eating is flexible. It varies in response to your emotions, your schedule, your hunger and your closeness to food," Love says in one of many handouts given to her patients.

    Page Love strives to understand the root of unhealthy eating habits and concludes that, "the conditions with food that we are raised with, how are family eats, or ethnic group eats or our friends" define the way we perceive food. "It also has a good bit to do with genetic compulsiveness. We know there are genetic ties to alcoholism, and now researchers are identifying similar genes for compulsive personality types in all eating disorders," Love says.

    Society identifies success with achieving an ideal weight, and Love finds many people ignore or suppress hunger in order to attain a false sense of power and control with weight loss. "I am of the belief that knowledge is power to then make an informed decision about your own health," Love says, "There are some people who believe that we shouldn't "put ideas" into young people's heads because it might cultivate the very behaviors we don't want them to participate in, but it's very much like sex or drug education." In addition to Love's tips and advice for young people, the resources provided on this page offer excellent outlets for anyone struggling with body image.

Love's patients learn to listen to his or her body and its physical cues of hunger, fullness, and sense of well-being, as well as taste. "If we are surrounded by family and friends who respect their body," Love says, "only say positive body statements, eat when they are hungry, stop when they are full, eat in regular intervals, and not judge occasional fun or emotional eating, the result is a healthier relationship with food and body."

*name has been changed to protect the identity of the student

ೞ

I know you have worked with the Olympic team and athletics the Atlanta Braves. I also know you have two passions: athletics and eating disorders. Could you call on all that experience and talk about Eileen's visits at Scripps and at Rhode Island Hospital? Specifically, what was your experience after Jeff asked for help? And could you identify which places are more accessible with less insurance problems?

271

My time with professional athletes introduced me to working with eating disorders. My 1st eating disorder client was an elite cross country runner with anorexia who was quite acute, experiencing sport injuries and fatty acid deficiencies. For the last 10 years, I have worked closely with the WTA, Women's International Tennis Association where I often see subclinical eating disorder symptoms seen in female athletes who experience overtraining/negative energy balance issues (very much like women with anorexia) – anemia, amenorrhea, low energy, stress fx, etc.

Eileen's experience in Rhode Island, Outpatient, I believe was much like the ACE program described above, so had limitations based on her acute status upon entering the program. Whenever clients return to home settings and lose the 24/7 support of ongoing medical care and all meals being provided, they often start to fall back into old patterns....eating rituals, missing meals, limiting food choices, over exercise, etc, so often they degrade quickly

Eileen's In Patient experience at Scripps was much more positive and b/c of the 24/7 supervision, groups, meal support, and medical support. Eileen thrived in this environment where she was able to weight restore significantly, challenge behaviors, and develop long term relationships with staff. This is often the case with long-term residential care for acute anorexic clients who can do longer term care stays of 3-6 mths. Eileen has thrived multiple times in this environment.

In my opinion where her treatment suffered was in stepping down from these types of programs … stepping down to too low of a level of care from intensive residential programs.

Working with Eileen's brother Jeff was a very positive experience. He was an extremely supportive family member from a distance working with Eileen when she lived in Atlanta. Unfortunately, her local brother, in Atlanta, who she was living with for a short time, was not as supportive. From an outsiders view it was like a Jekyll and Hyde situation for Eileen (Jeff was Jekyll). Jeff always stayed calm and supportive of Eileen's situation with her dying mother and wanting to support whatever level of support she needed. He seemed very open to my suggestions for her care and her living situation.

How do you approach chronic cases like Eileen?

A good example of how I deal with chronic cases such as Eileen can be seen in a recent piece I wrote about similar cases in "The Renfrew Perspective" where I address family relationships and dealing with death of acute clients I have had.

*Read this article by Page Love about a disordered eating case study, from **The Renfrew Center's** Perspectives newsletter…*
http://www.nutrifitga.com/upload/Nutritherapy/img0 30pdf.pdf

Eileen wants to make sure you understand the whole point of the book is that there is meaning to this disease and that you can replace that meaning with something life affirming rather than something demeaning and destructive. She believes in telling any family member that each person deserves to be loved, no matter the affliction. Unconditional love, a love that is not worried about 2nd or 3rd or 70th chances. Your comment?

I do believe it's important for families to offer unconditional love....I have seen so many clients thrive under that type of supportive environment vs the opposite. But, that being said, there still need to be reasonable limits so that families are not enabling clients ... to continue their same destructive patterns and not heal or recover.

Have you been exposed to the idea of Gentle Teaching and do you believe in its precepts?

I am not fully aware of a formalized Gentle Teaching therapeutic approach, but I do feel I utilize some of that...but I am also of a tough love philosophy background. There is no question Eileen is a gentle soul....and does well with this approach.

ReMUDa RaNCH
REVEAL | RENEW | RECOVER

1 W Apache St, Wickenburg,
AZ 85390, United States
+1 800-445-1900

Remuda Ranch understands the pain that eating disorders can bring. There is hope and we can help. Our experienced staff is here to help you or your loved one to the road recovery. For over twenty years Remuda Ranch has been helping people recover from eating disorders. There is hope. There is help. There is Remuda Ranch.

With two locations in scenic Arizona, Remuda Ranch is a beautiful place to start the healing process. Nestled within the heart of Arizona, our two state-of-the-art locations can provide for your medical and treatment needs, while providing the perfect place to heal and find hope.

For many years, Remuda Ranch was a popular dude ranch in the small town of Wickenburg, Arizona. In nineteen ninety, Ward Keller purchased Remuda Ranch with the intent of transforming it into a treatment center for women and girls with eating disorders. This was the result of experiencing a daughter with anorexia and seeing first-hand the need for excellent care. Remuda Ranch started with only a handful of patients and staff, but as eating disorders grew more prevalent, so did the size and scope of the company.

Today, Remuda Ranch treats women, teens and children with Anorexia, Bulimia, and related issues. Additionally, we treat those struggling with binge eating disorder, obesity, and compulsive overeating in our Binge Eating Disorder Program. We treat women, 18 and older, struggling with obsessive compulsive disorder (OCD), panic disorder, social anxiety disorder and body dysmorphic disorder.

If you or someone you know is suffering from an eating disorder, there is hope. We can help. Contact Remuda Ranch today and take that first important step towards the path of recovery.

AMERICAN ANOREXIA/BULIMIA ASSOCIATION (AABA)
165 W. 46TH ST., SUITE 1108
NEW YORK, NY 10036
(212) 575-6200

The American Anorexia Bulimia Association is a national, non-profit organization of concerned members of the public and healthcare industry dedicated to the prevention and treatment of eating disorders. Through education, advocacy and research, AABA serves as a national authority on eating disorders and related concerns. AABA promotes social attitudes that enhance healthy body image and works to overcome the idealization of thinness that contributes to disordered eating.

Our mission is carried out through many different services, including: help-lines, referral networks, public information, school outreach, media support, professional training, support groups and prevention programs.

Eileen Rand

NATIONAL EATING DISORDERS ORGANIZATION (NEDO)
6655 S. YALE AVE.
TULSA, OK 74136
(918) 481-4044

NEDA Network Members:

National Eating Disorders Association

Austin Foundation for Eating Disorders (AFED), Texas http://www.austinfed.org/

Community Outreach for the Prevention of Eating Disorders (COPE) http://www.cope-ecf.org/

Eating Disorders Coalition of Tennessee http://www.edct.net/

The Eating Disorder Foundation, Colorado http://www.eatingdisorderfoundation.org/

Eating Disorders Information Network (EDIN), Georgia http://www.myedin.org/

Eating Disorder Network of Central Florida http://www.edncf.com/

Eating Disorder Network (EDN) of Maryland http://www.ednmaryland.org/

Eating Disorders Resource Center (EDRC), California http://www.edrcsv.org/

The Elisa Project, Texas http://www.theelisaproject.org/

Helping Other People Eat (H.O.P.E.), Florida
http://www.hopetolive.com/

The Manna Scholarship Fund, Georgia
http://www.mannafund.org/

Maudsley Parents http://www.maudsleyparents.org/

MCR Foundation, Tennessee
http://www.mcrfoundation.com/

Michigan Eating Disorders Alliance
http://www.mieda.org/

Missouri Eating Disorders Association (Formerly
The Dahlia Partnership)
http://moeatingdisorders.org/

Multi-Service Eating Disorders Association, Inc.
(MEDA), Massachusetts http://www.medainc.org/

The National Association for Males with Eating
Disorders (NAMED) http://namedinc.org/

Oklahoma Eating Disorders Association (OEDA)
http://okeatingdisorders.org/

Ophelia's Place, New York http://opheliasplace.org/

Project Heal http://www.theprojectheal.org/

T.H.E Center for Disorders Eating, North Carolina
http://www.thecenternc.org/

Tri-State Eating Disorder Resource Team, Indiana
http://www.edrteam.org/

What We Do: NEDA is Feeding Hope.

The Challenge
In the United States, 20 million women and 10 million men suffer from a clinically significant eating disorder at some time in their life, including anorexia nervosa, bulimia nervosa, binge eating disorder, or an eating disorder not otherwise specified.

The scope and severity of eating disorders are often misunderstood. Eating disorders are serious illnesses, not lifestyle choices. In fact, anorexia has the highest mortality rate of any mental illness. In a national survey, four out of ten people reported that they either suffered or have known someone who has suffered from an eating disorder. There is a significant lack of funding to combat eating disorders and their devastating consequences. As a result, too many individuals and families are left feeling helpless, hopeless and frightened.

The Opportunity
We can confront these serious illnesses with increased awareness, early intervention and improved access to treatment. NEDA provides programs and services to give families the support they need to find answers for these life-threatening illnesses.

Recovery is possible. We are working to make it happen.

http://eatingdisorders.ucla.edu/default.cfm

Eileen Rand

**ANOREXIA NERVOSA AND RELATED
EATING DISORDERS INC. (ANRED)**
  P.O. BOX 5102
  EUGENE, OR 97405
  (541) 344-1144

We are a nonprofit organization that provides
information about anorexia nervosa, bulimia
nervosa, binge eating disorder, and other less-well-
known food and weight disorders. Our material
includes self-help tips and information about
recovery and prevention.

How to use the ANRED website

About fifty documents are available here.
Check the Table of Contents to see a list of the
topics we cover. Print out anything you like, and as
much as you like, but please do not change the pages
in any way. Also, if you use our material in a report,
paper, presentation, etc., please give us credit.

There are two easy ways you can find
information on the ANRED site.

Number one: Go to the Table of Contents.
Find the particular topic you want to learn about, and
click on the link that will take you to it.

Number two: Begin on the first page and read
straight through to the end of the site by clicking on
the Forward to the Next Page links at the bottom of
every page.

NATIONAL ASSOCIATION OF ANOREXIA NERVOSA AND ASSOCIATED DISORDERS (ANAD)
P.O. BOX 7, HIGHLAND PARK, IL 60035
(847) 831-3438

Get Help

If you think you or someone you know is battling an eating disorder, don't be afraid to talk to someone about it.

ANAD helpline (630) 577-1330, operates 9 AM-5 PM Central Time, Monday through Friday and can help you find the treatment to fit your needs. If you prefer email, please contact us through anadhelp@anad.org.
Holiday Hours: Wednesday, January 1st Closed

ANAD Support groups meet weekly, biweekly or monthly.

There are several levels of treatment for eating disorders, these include weekly support groups, outpatient treatment with a therapist, psychiatrist and dietitian, partial hospitalization, and finally inpatient or residential treatment. Our listings are for your consideration. We encourage you to screen these therapists for yourself and decide who is best for you. Also, our online list is not exhaustive.

Outpatient treatment might be meeting with a psychotherapist on a weekly basis. More intensive outpatient treatment might be weekly meetings with a psychotherapist, psychiatrist and dietitian, who all work together on your recovery. Finally, some hospitals have outpatient programs that meet five to seven days a week for a few hours and include individual psychotherapy, group psychotherapy and group meetings with the psychotherapist, psychiatrist, dietitian and other hospital staff.

Intensive Outpatient or IOP typically occurs in a specialized setting where clients will typically attend two or three times a week. Clients will have access to all the services in one location, which usually include individual therapy, nutritional therapy, family therapy, group therapy, and more.

Day Treatment or Partial Hospitalization are a step up from outpatient treatment, and most meet daily. They are generally eight to twelve hours of the day, and one or two structured/supported meals are provided at the facility. Clients will return home to sleep at night.

The most intense level of treatment is **Inpatient or Residential treatment.** This involves living in a residential facility or hospital and includes eating all meals, performing all daily activities, and a significant level of treatment individually and in groups.

Residential Treatment provides 24-hour care for those who are medically stable but who are still engaging in eating disorder behaviors. Intensive supervision and support are provided.

Inpatient Treatment is for those individuals who are in significant physical danger and/or medically unstable -24-hour care in a medical or psychiatric unit which is designed to handle medical complications, begin weight restoration, respond to other self-destructive behaviors, and begin psychological intervention.

Eileen Rand

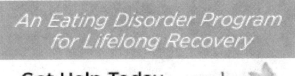

Publisher's Note

I have had the pleasure of working with Eileen Rand for the better part of a year. I was originally hired as a ghostwriter for a memoir of the lifelong Anorexic. But a funny thing happened along the way. Eileen and I became fast friends, and what was to be a professional work for a client became the collaboration of two peers. This progression shows up in the book as we turn away from chapters of monologue and begin an intimate session of questions and answers. Is the book better or worse for this occurrence? I think it's much improved, and it's my hope you'll be touched in some deep way by this open and sometimes horrific account of a lady who has spent 37 years battling a disease that just won't go away.

This being such a closely held work has also lead to my agreement to traditionally release the memoir through my publishing house Chase Enterprises Publishing.

Thank you for reading our book.

Chase Enterprises Publishing

Eileen Rand

End

CPSIA information can be obtained
at www.ICGtesting.com
Printed in the USA
FSOW02n1742150115
4478FS

9 781927 915066